SUCCESS AT THE ENQUIRY DESK

Other titles in the Successful LIS Professional series

THE SUCCESSFUL LIS PROFESSIONAL

SERIES EDITOR
Shella Pantry

Third edition

SUCCESS AT THE ENQUIRY DESK

Successful enquiry answering – every time

Tim Owen

LIBRARY ASSOCIATION PUBLISHING
LONDON

© Tim Owen 1996, 2000

Published by
Library Association Publishing
7 Ridgmount Street
London WC1E 7AE

Library Association Publishing is wholly owned by The Library Association.

First published 1996
First revised edition 1997
Second revised edition 1998
This third edition 2000

British Library Cataloguing in Publication Data
A catalogue record for this book is available from the British Library.

ISBN 1-85604-404-1

Typeset in 11/14 pt Aldine 721 by Library Association Publishing.
Printed and made in Great Britain by MPG Books Ltd, Bodmin, Cornwall.

Contents

Series Editor's preface

With rapid technological advances and new freedoms, the workplace presents a dynamic and challenging environment. It is just these advances, however, that necessitate a versatile and adaptable workforce which is aware that lifelong full-time jobs are a thing of the past. Work is being contracted out, de-structured organizations are emerging, and different skills and approaches are required from workers, who must solve new and changing problems. These workers must become self-motivated, multi-skilled and constantly learning. Demonstrating the international economic importance of professional development, the European Commission has officially voiced its support for a European community committed to lifelong learning.

For the information professional, the key to success in this potentially de-stabilizing context is to develop the new skills the workplace demands. Above all, the LIS professional must actively prioritize a commitment to continuous professional development. The information industry is growing fast and the LIS profession is experiencing very rapid change. This series has been designed to help you manage change by ensuring the growth of your own portfolio of professional skills. By reading these books you will have begun the process of seeing yourself as your own best resource and accepting the rewarding challenge of staying ahead of the game.

The series is very practical, focusing on specific topics relevant to all types of library and information service. Recognizing that your time is precious, these books have been written so that they may be easily read and digested. They include instantly applicable ideas and techniques which you can put to the test in your own workplace, helping you to succeed in your job.

The authors have been selected because of their practical experience and enthusiasm for their chosen topic and we hope you will benefit from their advice and guidance. The points for reflection, checklists and summaries are designed to provide stepping stones for you to assess your understanding of the topic as you read.

Anyone entering or already in the information profession will find it an exciting and, at times, a challenging profession, especially when dealing with customer enquiries. Information professionals are expected to know the answers to any type of question, and I know many who pride themselves on being able to find answers to the wide variety of often complex topics which our customers present to us on a daily basis.

Tim Owen's extremely successful and thought-provoking book, now in its third revised edition in four years, will introduce and guide you through techniques which help you to answer such enquiries logically and efficiently.

The fact that the first two editions of this book, and the training courses offered alongside it, are so successful, shows that it will be worth investing your time in reading *Success at the enquiry desk*. I am positive that you will find many new ways, including the efficient use of the Internet, to improve the quality and effectiveness of your enquiry answers. And don't forget that presentation of your answers also count: Tim offers guidance on ensuring that you do not spoil the end results.

Books in this series are intentionally short in length and are intended to help the busy professional, therefore they cannot deal with all situations in great detail, but the case studies play a valuable role in illustrating ideas, and in addition the lists of other information sources will allow the reader to follow up any point.

As an information professional who is extremely keen on professional development at any age I recommend this series to you. I am positive you will benefit from your investment!

Sheila Pantry OBE

Introduction

Each time I've come to revise this book I've started by saying 'There's never been a better time to be in the information profession', and each time it's been more true than before. Everywhere you look, television, radio, magazines and newspapers are talking about the world wide web, e-mail, new delivery platforms such as mobile phones and digital TV, the challenges of e-commerce and the opportunities offered by the information society. Information has a higher profile in government, business and society than ever before, and top information professionals can reap rich benefits in terms of status and salary.

Newcomers are entering the profession at a particularly exciting time. It's a growth industry, whose potential we are only just beginning to exploit. And, for longer established members, there are opportunities to be seized from developments such as the People's Network, electronic government and knowledge management. For better or worse, the Internet has changed everything.

But some things don't change. Medieval monks in chained libraries wrestled with exactly the same problems as online searchers do today – how to satisfy your enquirer with the right information, at the right level, on time. The only difference is that we now have infinitely more flexible tools with which to do the job.

This book will help you to do that job more efficiently. It's not a dressed-up bibliography – it's an introduction to techniques that can help you deal with enquiries on any subject, whether or not there are publications about it. These techniques make use of the web where appropriate, but they meld it with other sources, both printed and electronic. The examples used in the book largely reflect my own experience in social science, current affairs and business information. But the techniques work just as effectively for enquiries about technology, medicine, arts or law. Certainly you'll need to have a few key sources always at your fingertips, but that's not what enquiry answering is about.

Nor does this book shroud things in mystery or jargon, or pretend that things are more complicated than they really are. It's just applied common sense. Anyone, with or without a library or information qualification, can become self-sufficient when it comes to finding things out. Indeed, as more and more emphasis is laid on information handling skills in formal education, and growing numbers of people engage in self-directed lifelong learning, then techniques such as these will become more widespread across the population as a whole.

Our job as information professionals is to refine those skills even further, so that when our enquirers are finally at a loss, we are still able to offer them more help. So what this book will do is take you through all the various stages of answering an enquiry. It will warn you of the pitfalls to avoid – misunderstanding the question, providing too much information. It will help you with ideas for what to do when you can't find the answer. And when you are finally successful, it will show you how you can increase your job satisfaction, and enhance the reputation of your library or information service, by adding value to the answer.

Exciting prospects await anyone fortunate enough to be in the library and information business at this time. But you can't exploit them without grasping the basic principles first. I hope this short book will prove helpful as you pursue your career in one of the world's most fascinating occupations.

Tim Owen

Ten steps to successful enquiry answering: The *Success at the enquiry desk* enquiry form

Enquiry forms come in all shapes and sizes. At their most basic, they may simply have somewhere to record the question and the enquirer's contact details, followed by a large blank space for you to use as you wish. More complex forms may require you to record your search strategy, or even include suggestions for sources you could try. In some commercial information broking services, enquiries are recorded electronically, to provide an audit trail for charging purposes. Other libraries and information units don't use forms at all, but rely on notebooks or even scrap paper.

Our enquiry form (on the next two pages) tries to give you as much help as possible. In ten steps, it takes you through the entire process, from recording the question to the final sign-off, when the enquiry has been answered successfully and you are considering what follow-up action the enquiry may require – recording a useful new reference source in your information file, for example, or a new website that you could bookmark as a favourite for future use. At steps 4 and 6, we make suggestions on possible sources you could try – first types of source, and then some actual titles. We make sure that you analyse the enquiry accurately (step 3), and that you plan your search strategy properly (step 5). In fact, our enquiry form follows the structure of this book.

We've had to compress it to fit it onto the book's small pages (you'd certainly need a lot more space for sections 7 and 8), and what you see as a pair of facing pages would actually be the front and back of the form. All the same, you may like to adapt it for use in your own library or information unit.

1 QUESTION (as much detail as possible)	2 ENQUIRER DETAILS
	Name:
	Organization:
	Address:
	Postcode:
	Tel:
	Fax:
Enquiry taken by:	E-mail:
Deadline:	Special contact instructions:

3 ENQUIRY ANALYSIS	4 ENQUIRY TYPE
	Focus...
Who?	Broad: ❑ Narrow: ❑
What?	**Dyanamism...**
When?	Static: ❑ Dynamic: ❑
Where?	**Complexity...**
Why?	Single issue: ❑ Multi-faceted: ❑
How?	**Viability...**
	Can't be answered in-house: ❑
What will the final answer look like?	Not available in a published source: ❑
	(See over for possible types of source to use)

5 SEARCH STRATEGY	6 POSSIBLE STARTER SOURCES
Search terms:	(See over for suggestions)
Broader terms:	
Narrower terms:	
Related terms:	
(N.B. Consider American spellings and terminology)	

7 SOURCES TRIED	8 SEARCH RESULTS

9 ANSWER	10 SIGN-OFF
	Enquiry completed by:
	Answer delivered by:
	Success...
	Complete: ❑ Partial: ❑ Compromise: ❑
	Enquiry referred to:
	Time taken to answer: ....hrs ....mins
	Delivered on time? Yes: ❑ No: ❑
	Reasons if late:
	Follow-up action (eg add new information or source to information file):

TYPES OF SOURCE TO CONSIDER (Section 4)	POSSIBLE STARTER SOURCES (Section 6)
Broad Entry in a general encyclopaedia Chapter in a textbook Complete textbook	**Comprehensive facts & figures** *Whitaker's almanac* *Britain . . . the official yearbook of the UK*
Narrow Entry in a special encyclopaedia Index entry in a textbook Special report Periodical article Table in a statistical journal Entry in a directory Database record Web page	**Events & dates** *Keesing's record of world events* *Annual register* **Statistics** *Annual abstract of statistics* *Regional trends* *Social trends*
Static Encyclopaedia or dictionary Textbook Selection of periodical articles Statistical time series Directory CD-ROM database	**Finding contacts for further information** *Directory of British associations* *Councils, committees & boards* *Aslib directory of information sources in the United Kingdom* *Guide to libraries & information units in government departments & other organisations*
Dynamic Current newspaper Recent periodical Latest statistical journal Press release Online news service – proprietary or web Audiotex	*Hollis UK press & public relations annual* *World of learning* **Identifying reference sources** *Walford's guide to reference material* *Current British directories*
Single issue Printed source if easy to find Database/Web if hard to find	**Identifying periodicals** *Willing's press guide* *Benn's media*
Multi-faceted Online database/web CD-ROM database	**Identifying statistical sources** *Guide to official statistics* *Sources of unofficial UK statistics*
Can't be answered in-house Library or information unit guide Nearby public or educational library Personal contact	**Tracing books** *Books in English* *Bowker/Whitaker global books in print on disc*
Not available in a published source Specialist organization Author of nearly relevant publication Editor of relevant periodical Personal contact	**Tracing articles** *British humanities index* *Abstracts in new technologies and engineering* *Clover information index* **Tracing news items** *Clover newspaper index*

Twenty-five multi-purpose reference sources you can't afford to ignore

Ever since you were a child at school, you've been looking things up - using encyclopaedias, dictionaries, phone books, recipe books, *Who's whos*. By now you'll also be familiar with your own library's catalogue and any internal information files that the staff may have compiled. You'll know about your library's CD-ROMs of reference works, newspapers, periodicals or statistics, and you'll probably have access to the world wide web. In other words, you already know a great deal about how to find information.

But for really successful enquiry work, there's a small core of more specialist reference sources that it's worth knowing about. On the next page you'll find a quick checklist of some of the most useful ones, and there are full bibliographic details of these and other sources, with annotations, starting on page 73.

Almost all of these sources are available in printed form; many are also on CD-ROM, and more and more are appearing on the web too. Usually web versions of reference sources will be password-protected, commercially priced services, but some – including *Encyclopaedia Britannica* (**http://www.britannica.com**) – are available free of charge. You can also expect to find increasing numbers of websites that bring together related reference sources into single products for convenience as one stop shop information services. Examples of this are the commercial services *KnowUK* (**http://www.knowuk.co.uk/**) and *KnowEurope* (**http://www. knoweurope.net/**) and the Government statistical compilation *Statbase* (**http://www.statistics.gov.uk**).

It's difficult to carry too many sources of this kind in your head – 25 seems a good number to start with. So try to become familiar with them (and their international equivalents); they'll get you started on a great many of the enquiries you'll have to deal with.

Purpose	Item number	Title	International equivalents
Comprehensive facts & figures	1	Whitaker's almanac	Europa world yearbook
	2	Britain ... the official yearbook of the United Kingdom	Statesman's yearbook
Events & dates	3	Keesing's record of world events	[Keesing's record of world events]
	4	Annual register	[Annual register]
Statistics	5	Annual abstract of statistics	United Nations statistical yearbook
			Eurostat: basic statistics of the European Union
	6	Regional trends	
	7	Social trends	World marketing data & statistics
Finding contacts for further information	8	Directory of British associations	Encyclopaedia of associations: international organizations
			Europa directory of international organizations
			Yearbook of international organizations
			Pan European associations
			Directory of European industrial & trade associations
			Directory of European professional & learned societies
	9	Councils, committees & boards	
	10	Aslib directory of information sources in the United Kingdom	
	11	Guide to libraries & information units in government departments & other organisations	
	12	Hollis UK press & public relations annual	Hollis Europe: the directory of European public relations & PR networks
	13	World of learning	[World of learning]
Identifying reference sources	14	Walford's guide to reference material	
	15	Current British directories	Ulrich's international periodicals directory (incorporating irregular serials & annuals)
Identifying periodicals	16	Willing's press guide	[Willing's]
	17	Benn's media	[Benn's]
			Ulrich's international periodicals directory (incorporating irregular serials & annuals)
Identifying statistical sources	18	Guide to official statistics	Instat: international statistics sources
	19	Sources of unofficial UK statistics	World directory of non-official statistical sources
			Statistics Europe
Tracing books	20	Books in English	[Books in English]
	21	Bowker/Whitaker global books in print on disc	[Bowker/Whitaker global books in print on disc]
Tracing articles	22	British humanities index	Humanities abstracts
			Social sciences index
	23	Abstracts in new technologies and engineering	Applied science index & abstracts
			General science abstracts
	24	Clover information index	
Tracing news items	25	Clover newspaper index	Keesing's record of world events

Chapter 1
What do you really want?

How to make sure you really understand the question

In this chapter you'll find out how to:

➤ avoid misunderstandings
➤ ask the right questions
➤ agree the task
➤ find out how long you've got to do it

There's a story told of a London taxi driver some years ago who picked up an American fare outside Victoria Station. There was a big Egyptology exhibition on at the British Museum at the time. 'Take me to Tutankhamun,' the lady drawled. So the cabbie did. Thirty minutes later he dropped her at a rather down-at-heel patch of open space in the south-west London suburbs, called 'Tooting Common'.

It's an apocryphal tale, no doubt. But it does show the problems you can hit when dealing with what seems like the simplest of enquiries. Most of your queries are likely to come orally – face-to-face or over the phone. The possibilities for misunderstandings are endless – accent, articulation, assumptions – all can send you scurrying off in totally the wrong direction, wasting both your time and the enquirer's. So the first task has to be – make sure you understand the question.

Avoiding misunderstandings

Remember when you were doing your exams, and teachers and lecturers dinned into you the lesson 'read the whole paper first'? Well, it matters just as much here. Because, if you get it wrong, it'll be your fault no matter how unhelpful the enquirer has been. You are the professional, remember, and the enquirer is the amateur.

Just think of all the different types of enquirer you might meet, and the things that could go wrong as a result . . .

Type 1: The homophone victim

I'm looking for information on migration patterns in whales

means:

I'm looking for information on migration patterns in Wales

Type 2: The Chinese whisperer

Could you tell me how I can join the Envy Queue?

means:

Could you tell me how I can gain an NVQ?

Type 3: The malapropist

Do you have the Electrical Register?

means:

Do you have the electoral register?

Type 4: The generalist

Do you have any books on retailing?

means:

What is Marks & Spencer's current pretax profit?

Type 5: The know-all

I need some statistics from Employment gazette.

means:

I need earnings data for female employees in Croydon; I'm guessing that they're in Employment gazette *because I don't want to seem ignorant.* [Actually, they aren't. And it hasn't been called *Employment gazette* for years, but *Labour market trends.*]

Type 6: The muddler

Have you got any books on Kew Gardens? That's to say, something on the Crystal Palace, if you can manage it. What would be really helpful, actually, would be the index to the Illustrated London news. *Or, better still, a book on tropical fish.*

means:

I'm doing a project on the Westminster Aquarium.

Type 7: The obsessively secretive

Where's the catalogue?

means (after a lot of tactful questioning):

I know there have been reports in the papers that MPs have been accepting cash in return for asking Parliamentary questions, and that one paper has actually named names; I'm very concerned about this because my brother is an MP and he may be involved because he's been asking questions about immigration quotas and he's sponsored by the Strong & Moral Britain Association, which I think is associated with neo-fascist organizations; can you confirm this, or let me know where its funding comes from? I really need to know because I'm about to become a governor of a school with a large number of Asian children – so I'd also like to find out what obligation there is on school governors to declare other interests, but I don't want to approach the school directly about this in case they start asking awkward questions.

Some of these are real examples, some exaggerations. (The last one is almost a total fiction.) But they all pose real dangers. Rule number one of enquiry answering is that people almost never ask the question they really want to know the answer to.

Disgruntled and unconvinced enquirers

There are all sorts of reasons for this. They may not want to bother the busy librarian. It's true, a big public or educational library can be a busy place. You can have people queuing up at the enquiry desk just when Maisie decides to go off for coffee. When you're under pressure, it's always a temptation to take an enquiry at face value and answer the ques-

3

tion actually put to you. Resist it! You're almost certain to have a disgruntled customer returning to the enquiry desk before too long, and that's a waste of everybody's time, and really bad public relations.

Equally alarming is the kind of enquirer who lacks confidence in your ability to answer the question. They'd sooner browse themselves, perhaps inefficiently, than risk having their time wasted by you. This kind should be sending alarm signals both to you and to your boss. It probably means that the enquirer has had bad experiences before – either at your library or somewhere else. Either way, it's up to you to convince them, quickly, that you can help, even if you don't know anything about the subject they are interested in. This doesn't mean trying to pull the wool over their eyes – that's the worst possible tactic. You're bound to get found out, and you'll just reinforce the enquirer's scepticism. There are ways of being helpful, even if you haven't a clue what the enquirer is talking about.

Secretive enquirers and time-wasters

Thirdly, there are enquirers who just don't want anyone to know what they're doing. These can be the most infuriating kind. Despite your gentle persuasion, they resolutely refuse to disclose any information that might help you to help them. But you must suppress your urge to get annoyed. That will only make matters worse. They may have excellent reasons for not wanting to give anything away. It might be someone applying for a job with a big local firm who doesn't want their current employer to get wind of it. It might be an academic who doesn't want to be beaten to publication by a rival. Or would *you* want everyone to know that you were looking for addresses of HIV clinics?

Finally, there are time wasters – people who want to burden you with every tiny detail of their investigation, together with the complete life stories of all their sisters, cousins and aunts. Genealogical enquirers frequently fall into this category. You owe it to your other enquirers to steer this type to the point as quickly as possible. They'll try to persuade you that you can't possibly help them without a full understanding of their needs. They may genuinely believe this, or they may simply have time on their hands, and be looking for someone to talk to. Either way, you have to focus them, tactfully.

There are ways of dealing with all these types. You'll need to be approachable, reassuring, discreet and tactful. Above all, you need to maintain what the police used to call an attitude of 'suspicious alertness'. You have to find out what you need to know by asking questions, and there are several different questioning techniques that you can employ. This is sometimes rather pretentiously referred to as 'the reference interview', but that implies a formality about the process that can be off-putting for the enquirer. It's really just about applying common sense.

Asking the right questions

One of the most useful things you can learn to do in enquiry work is to get into the habit of always asking a supplementary question. Practise it in conversation until it becomes second nature. It can provide an enormous number of clues as to what your enquirer really wants – and can sometimes reveal something completely unexpected that can prevent you from darting off in the wrong direction. Here's a silly example – you're in the kitchen and you think your partner said, 'Have you got the time?' So you reply, 'Do you mean what time is it now or how long does it take to cook?' 'No, no,' your partner answers, 'Did you remember to buy the thyme?'

You need different kinds of questions for different situations, different techniques for dealing with each of the types of enquirer listed above. Let's run through them, and the situations in which you might use them.

Open questions

These invite the enquirer to supply further details without your specifying what additional information would be helpful. You might need to use an open question to deal with a type 4 enquirer (the generalist). Perhaps something like 'Are you interested in any particular aspect of retailing?' And it may be your only way forward with type 7 (the obsessively secretive) with a response like 'I could give you a hand if you can give me an idea of what subject you're interested in.' However, open questions do have the disadvantage of leaving far too many options open.

Closed questions

These force the enquirer to give you a yes/no answer. With type 5 (the know-all) you might be tempted to ask, 'Are you sure that the statistics you want are published there?' But, if the know-all runs true to type, the answer will undoubtedly be 'Yes,' and you will have learned nothing. So you should use closed questions only when you are certain what the options are. For example, you could ask type 3 (the malapropist) 'Do you want the current register for this area?' (see below – 'Who, What, When, Where, Why, How?').

Forced choice questions

These force the enquirer to choose between alternatives. The little kitchen sink drama above uses a forced choice question. Or you might ask a type 1 enquirer (the homophone victim), 'Do you mean the sea creatures or the country?' They can be very helpful – they immediately narrow the field in a way that is being firmly directed by you. But you have to learn to think quickly to come up with two really useful options. You sometimes have to be tactful with forced choice questions too. After all, it's perfectly clear to the enquirer what he or she wants!

Multiple questions

These offer the enquirer a range of options to choose from. You'd use a multiple question when you're really not sure at all what the enquirer wants and you need to fish for ideas. An alternative might be to use an open question, but multiple-choice questions are likely to be much more useful, provided you can think quickly enough to come up with some sensible options. Instead of using an open question for type 4 (the generalist), you could try, 'Are you looking for information on retail management, shop design or location, market research, special types of retailer such as food or electrical goods shops – or even one particular retailer?' The only real problem with multiple questions is that you might confuse the enquirer by offering too many options. So it's worth considering asking a succession of forced-choice questions instead, moving from the general to the particular.

Leading questions

These lead the enquirer in the direction of the answer you want. You should only use them when you're 99% certain you do know what the enquirer wants. They can be dangerous, because they impose your assumptions on the enquirer's request, when what you really need to be sure of is that you haven't made any false assumptions. With type 1 (the homophone victim), you might ask, 'So it's *statistics* on their movements that you're looking for then?' Your enquirer might answer 'Yes', and be quite right. But you still don't know whether it's 'whales' or 'Wales'.

Hypothetical questions

These attempt to glean further information by putting a hypothetical situation to the enquirer. As with the multiple questions, you have to be able to think on your feet to come up quickly with a sensible hypothetical question. But they might be your only hope with type 6 (the muddler) because there's one hypothetical question that allows you to ask *the* forbidden question. You're not allowed to ask, 'What do you really want?' That sounds aggressive and suspicious and sends out the wrong signals to the enquirer. But you can put the same question in a hypothetical form by asking 'What would your *ideal* answer look like?' (We'll come back to this in Chapter 3.)

Agreeing the task

Whichever questioning technique you employ, the aim is the same. It's to find out, beyond any doubt, exactly what your enquirer wants you to do for them. For this you must be in full possession of the facts. Your chosen questioning strategy should allow you to do one or both of two things – funnelling and probing.

Funnelling focuses the enquirer in from the general to the particular. It would probably help with types 4 (the generalist) and 6 (the muddler). However it can also be an efficient way of dealing with the ambiguities offered by types 1 (the homophone victim), and 5 (the know-all). It's

7

usually the easier of the two techniques to apply because it needn't sound over inquisitive or threatening. Closed, forced choice and leading questions are all suitable for funnelling operations – although you should bear in mind that each of these techniques carries its own hazards. Forced choice is almost always the most efficient one.

Probing seeks further details from the enquirer when you're not at all clear what they want; you would use the technique to try to find out the context in which the enquirer was thinking. It might help you with types 2 (the Chinese whisperer) or 4 (the generalist), and you'll certainly need to deploy this technique with type 7 (the obsessively secretive). But you have to exercise caution and tact when using it, because it can sound inquisitorial. Open, multiple and hypothetical questions might all help you to probe. On the whole, multiple questions are probably best here – they don't sound so inquisitorial, they show that you're trying to help and taking the enquiry seriously, and they're more likely to put the enquirer at their ease than on their guard.

Who, what, when, where, why, how?

'I keep six honest serving men – they taught me all I knew,' said Kipling in the *Just so* stories. To answer any enquiry effectively, you need them too; they are the six questions – Who? What? When? Where? Why? How? Your enquirer will fill in some of the blanks relatively unprompted – once you've discovered what they really want, of course, as opposed to what they begin by asking. Your supplementary questioning should either fill in or eliminate the others.

➤ Who? *might mean* What kinds of people, animals, organizations are we dealing with?
➤ What? *might mean* What are those people, animals or organizations doing? *or* What do you, the enquirer, want to do with the information?
➤ When? *might mean* Are we dealing with current, recent or historical information?
➤ Where? *might mean* Which localities, regions, countries do we have to consider?

➤Why? *might mean* Why are they doing it? *or* Why are you, the enquirer, interested in this subject?

➤How? *might mean* What methods are they using to do it? *or* How do you, the enquirer, want the subject handled?

You wouldn't necessarily always take the questions in this order. (Kipling didn't.) Your enquirer's answers would fill in the blanks for some of them as you went along. Sometimes your questions will seek to elicit more information about the subject requested, and at other times you will be looking for information on why the enquirer is interested and how s/he wants the subject handled.

Let's see how it might work for some of the questions to which our enquirers above really wanted answers.

Type 1: The homophone victim

I'm looking for information on migration patterns in whales

So we need something like a big animal encyclopaedia then? (**Who** are we looking for?)

Oh, sorry – you mean people in Wales moving around? (**What** are they doing?)

Do you mean things like how they travel to work, or what they do when they move house? (**How** are they doing it?)

Is it just movements within the country, or from outside as well? (**Where** do we have to consider?)

Are you looking for information on why people move – or just the figures? (**Why** do you need the information?)

Are you looking just for movements now – or back over a period? (**When** do we have to consider?)

I'm looking for information on migration patterns in Wales

Verdict: Once you've got over the initial misunderstanding, you should be able to get all the way with this enquiry – it's precise and specific.

Type 4: The generalist

Do you have any books on retailing?

Yes, is it one particular retailer? (**Who** are we looking for?)

So it's Marks & Spencer; are you looking for financial information or news on the company's activities? (**What** do you need to know about them?)

So you need the latest accounts? (**When** are you interested in?)

Just its UK operation, or worldwide? (**Where** do we need to consider?)

Is it detailed information for investment purposes, or just a brief financial profile for information? (**Why** do you need the information?)

Do you need the figures in manipulable form? On a CD-ROM? (**How** do you want the information presented?)

What is Marks & Spencer's current pretax profit?

Verdict: This may be an over optimistic scenario. Enquirers can be extraordinarily secretive about money matters, and here we reached the crucial company name remarkably fast. After that, however, the thing to bear in mind is that there is an enormous amount of business information available and it's easy to bury an enquirer under a deluge of semi-relevant information. So it's worth probing to find out precisely what they want.

Type 6: The muddler

Have you got any books on Kew Gardens? That's to say, something on the Crystal Palace, if you can manage it. What would be really helpful, actually, would be the index to the Illustrated London news. *Or, better still, a book on tropical fish.*

That's a wide range of topics; is there a common factor? (**Who** (or what subject) are you interested in?)

So it's information on zoos; would it actually be aquariums? (**What** kind of zoos?)

Victorian ones? (**When** would this be?)

And is it particularly London you're interested in? (**Where** are these aquariums?)

Are you trying to do a general history of aquariums? (**Why** do you want the information?)

So you want to concentrate on one aquarium; which one would that be? (**How** do you want the enquiry to proceed?)

I'm doing a project on the Westminster Aquarium.

Verdict: Like type 4, this is probably an over-optimistic scenario. The true muddler would probably go on muddling for some time before giving you the opportunity to start funnelling. But one advantage that muddlers offer over generalists or the obsessively secretive is that they do at least give you plenty of clues.

Type 7: The obsessively secretive

Where's the catalogue?

We have an online catalogue but it only covers the books; can I help further? (**How** can I help you?)

So it's something in the newspapers? (**What** sort of information do you need?)

Do you know roughly when? (**When** should we start looking?)

Can I help you with the CD-ROM? What subject are you interested in? (**What** kind of information do you need?)

So it's the cash for questions affair – would you like me to narrow the search down after that? (**How** would you like the enquiry to proceed?)

Ah, if it's a particular organization you want, a directory might actually help you better, or it might even have a website. (**Who** are you looking for?)

So you actually want something on how it's funded? Well, if it doesn't seem to have a website, let's see if we can find an article on it. (**What** is being done to this organization?)

Is it the race relations aspect you're interested in? For any particular purpose? (**Why** do you need the information?)

So it's school governorships? Sorry, I don't understand the connection with the cash for questions issue. (**Why** do you need to know this?)

It's a family connection? So it's a question of possible conflict of interest? (**How** are the two issues linked?)

So we're looking for something like the rules for school governors? (**How** do you want the subject handled?)

Cash for Parliamentary questions . . . Strong & Moral Britain Association . . . neo-fascist organizations . . . funding . . . school governors . . . declarations of interest.

Verdict: Like type 6, this is a somewhat compressed scenario. It would probably take a lot of very tactful questioning to elicit all the aspects of this complex and sensitive affair. Restricting your questioning to sources and techniques, as opposed to the specific information required, will probably reassure your enquirer. Then you can use your demonstration of how the source works to find out more about what your enquirer actually wants.

Keeping good records

As you can see from these examples, some of your questions come out as requests for further information, others as reactions to information received. That's how it usually happens in real life; the responses to either type will help you to fill in more of the blanks. If it's an oral enquiry, now is the time to repeat back to your enquirer what you think s/he wants you to do. Which brings us to the question of record-keeping.

Many libraries use pre-printed enquiry forms, and these can be laid out in innumerable different ways. (There's an example on page x designed especially for the techniques suggested in this book.) They can allow you not only to record the enquiry, but also to list the sources checked and the time taken, record any use of online databases and keep track of charges. They can also provide valuable performance data on the degree of success achieved, and alert your organization to any new information or sources that might be useful to your colleagues in the future. For the moment, though, you'll be using the form to ensure that you really do understand what your enquirer wants. Something like . . .

➤ *So we're looking for figures on how people have moved into, out of and within Wales between the 1981 and 1991 Censuses?*

➤ *So you just need a single figure – Marks & Spencer's latest pretax profit?*

➤ *So we're looking for anything we can find on the Westminster Aquarium, which was demolished some time in the late nineteenth or early twentieth century?*

➤ *So we need: something on the funding of the Strong & Moral Britain Association; information on whatever rules affect school governors; and it would help to have something from the papers on the cash-for-questions affair?*

Note the use of the word 'we'. This is your problem now, as well as your enquirer's, and it is only good customer relations to make that clear by involving yourself in it.

Finding out how long you've got

Finally, you have to agree a deadline. Often, this will be 'now'. The enquirer will be standing there, and they'll want you to point them in the right direction straight away. (We'll deal with techniques for thinking on your feet in Chapter 3.) But, if the enquiry has come in by phone, fax, letter or e-mail, you need to be quite clear when the answer is required by. So don't take 'As soon as possible' or 'It's urgent' for an answer. 'As soon as possible' could mean next year, from your point of view, and urgency can be measured in minutes or days. So politely pin your enquirer down to a date and/or time. And if you think the timescale is unrealistically short, don't say 'Can't be done' – keep it positive. Explain that you will only be able to provide a limited answer in that time, and invite your enquirer to extend the deadline. More often than not, you'll find that s/he is able to give you more time. (We'll deal with meeting deadlines in Chapter 6.)

You now have nearly all the information you need to tackle the enquiry. But you still have to find out just one more thing – how much information your enquirer wants, and in what detail. Until comparatively recently, information on many topics was a scarce commodity. But increasingly now, we're facing information overload, so whereas in the past it may simply have been a question of giving your enquirer whatever you could find, now you must have the courage to select and reject.

To recap . . .

➤ Beware of the pitfalls presented by homophone victims, Chinese whisperers, malapropists, generalists, know-alls, muddlers and the obsessively secretive.

➤ Employ open, closed, forced choice, multiple, leading or hypothetical questions, as appropriate.

➤ Look for answers to the questions Who? What? When? Where? Why? How?

➤ Don't accept a vague deadline.

Information overload is such an important topic that we're going to devote an entire chapter to it. So in Chapter 2, we'll look at how to provide the right amount of information – not too little, not too much.

Chapter 2
Not too much, now
Too much information is as bad as too little

In this chapter you'll find out how to:

➤ recognize the dangers of information overload
➤ discover how much information your enquirer needs
➤ work out the level of specialism
➤ begin earmarking and eliminating potential sources

There was once a little girl who was given a book to read as a homework project. At the end she had to write a report saying what she thought of it. So she did. She wrote 'This book tells me more than I wanted to know about penguins.'

Bear those penguins in mind as we move to the next stage of successful enquiry answering. (First of all, though, remember a key lesson from Chapter 1 – are they Antarctic sea birds, paperback books or chocolate biscuits?) But what really matters, here, is the lesson about 'more than I wanted to know'. If you think that finding information is hard, then rejecting it is even harder. It takes a lot of confidence to say to yourself, 'Now I've found it I realize I don't need it even though it's relevant.' There's always the nagging fear that you might be rejecting the one piece of information that your enquirer would have leapt at as the answer to all their problems. Of course, this shouldn't happen if you've done your questioning properly because, as well as discovering exactly what information is needed, you should also have discovered how much, and at what level.

Only a few years ago, this wasn't an issue. In many cases, you found whatever there was to find in the one or two printed sources available to you, handed them over, and the enquirer probably then had the job of modifying their demands in the light of whatever you had been able to come up with. But the computer has changed all that. All of a sudden we've gone from a situation where information was a scarce resource, to be husbanded and cropped carefully, to a glut, in which it grows and reproduces almost unchecked, threatening to overwhelm us in an impenetrable jungle. There's a phrase for this – information overload.

Information overload

Twenty years ago, if you wanted to find a piece of information that you thought had been in the newspapers, there was really only one place you could go – *The Times index*. Assuming that you were able to negotiate the somewhat eccentric indexing of our great newspaper of record successfully, you then had the option of actually looking up the story in *The Times* (probably on microfilm, a severe delaying factor in itself) or taking the dates as a basis and scanning through other newspapers for coverage of the same issue. *The Times index* came out several times a year – very late – and cumulated only into comparatively short periods, so unless you had a pretty clear idea of the dates you needed, you could easily consume the whole time allotted to your enquiry using this one retrieval tool only and still fail to find the information.

There were some alternative sources you could try. The indexing of *Keesing's contemporary archives* (now *Keesing's record of world events*) was somewhat more efficient, and it cumulated more quickly. But *Keesing's* is an international source, containing far less information than a run of newspapers covering the same period. So if the story you were looking for covered a United Kingdom issue of comparatively little international importance, then *Keesing's* probably wouldn't help. You could also try *British humanities index* if you thought the issue might have been the subject of comment in contemporary journals, or the extremely basic *Research index* if it were a business matter. But both of these sources are highly selective in their coverage of the titles they index. By and large therefore, your chances of failing to find the answer were pretty high.

Multiple media

Now just think how all that has changed. If you're searching for information in the newspapers now, you're more likely to be using a CD-ROM than a printed index. This gives you virtually instantaneous access to any word, any phrase, or any combination of words and phrases in your chosen newspaper title – and *all* the UK broadsheets are available, not just *The Times*. Of course, CD-ROM versions of newspapers each cover only a fairly limited period – a year or so as a rule. But if you're not sure of your dates, you can use the *Clover newspaper index* on CD-ROM or on the web; this allows you to search only on subject headings and the original headlines, but even this gives you infinitely more scope than *The Times index*, and it covers a much longer span of time at one go. Most newspapers have their own websites, giving access to recent stories and frequently to an archive as well – ft.com is probably the best known. Rolls-Royce services, such as FT Discovery, Lexis-Nexis, Factiva or Profound will allow you to do precise, complex searches on newspapers, wire services and articles for years back.

Of course, Rolls-Royces don't come cheap, but the web does, and that contains an almost unstoppable slurry of information, good and useless. What matters is the vast increase in the amount of information that it's now feasible to store, and the infinitely greater variety of ways in which you can retrieve it. So, whereas a few years ago you'd be lucky to find *anything* on most subjects, you now have a pretty good chance of finding *everything*. And that's almost certainly too much.

How much does your enquirer need?

So the last stage in your questioning is to find out more or less how much information your enquirer needs. A few years ago, 'Whatever you can find' was frequently the only realistic option. Now it's increasingly the least realistic one. You have the tools to bombard your enquirers with information, but you're not helping them if you do this, because they're looking to you not only to find the information they need but also to filter it, so they have enough to do whatever they want to do – no more, no less. So you need to employ the same questioning techniques that we discussed in Chapter 1, and several question types will do.

You could simply ask an open question – 'How much information do you need?' But you might not get a very precise answer – 'Whatever you can find' doesn't really help you very much. Also some enquirers might feel daunted by the task of trying to imagine for themselves what the final answer might look like. That's your job. So a multiple question might be better – something like 'Do you just want a few main points in note form, or a page or so of information, or something like an article, or a complete book?' This of course assumes that you have a fair idea of the form in which the information is likely to appear. But if it's a highly technical subject, or the enquirer has used terminology that is unfamiliar to you, you might not know what to expect. So a third possibility might be to put the hypothetical question 'What would your ideal answer look like?' This again puts the onus back on the enquirer, so it's to be avoided if at all possible. But it may be your only hope if your enquirer has really taken you into totally unfamiliar territory. (Whether or not you ask the *enquirer* this question, it's an absolutely crucial one that you need to ask *yourself* – as we shall see in Chapter 3.)

Whatever the enquirer answers – and, in this case, the multiple question is likely to elicit the most helpful answer, from your point of view – you should now have a clear idea of the kinds of sources to go to first. It may seem obvious, but it is vitally important to go to the best source first. (We'll deal with sources in the next couple of chapters.) If it gives you the answer you want, you can quite simply stop looking. It doesn't matter whether more information can be found elsewhere; once you have found enough to satisfy your enquirer's needs you should stop. This isn't being lazy – it's practical.

Information for a purpose

Firstly, once you've found enough to meet one enquirer's needs, you can move on to the next one. That way, no-one is kept waiting longer than they have to. Secondly, people rarely want information merely to satisfy their curiosity – they almost always need it for a purpose. Let's think about two of the commonest – school or college projects, and retirement hobbies.

However much you may privately regret a student's lack of curiosity, or deplore the narrow focus of a curriculum that forces this attitude upon them, you have to be realistic about it. You're not helping the hapless student or school child at all if you don't take a pragmatic approach. The fact is that they need enough information to allow them to get a good mark, and once they've got that, they can't afford the time to go browsing for more information because they've probably got three or four more projects or homework assignments coming up to deadline too. So help them to find what they want, and then when they've got enough – stop.

Retirement hobbyists, on the other hand, may be operating at the opposite extreme. They're delighted with every additional snippet of detail you can provide – even if they've read it in half a dozen other sources already. The danger here, of course, is that – in the nicest possible way – they can be terrible time-wasters. Whether you actually get carried along by their enthusiasm, or simply can't shake them off, you have to be systematic about your choice of sources to help them too – and the order of priority in which you use them. In both these cases, the aim is to help your enquirer become self-sufficient as rapidly as possible – to give them something to read, and get them settled down reading it.

Do-it-yourself?

Finally, you have to know just how much help to give. Teachers and lecturers are notorious at handing out projects with no thought whatsoever for the ease or difficulty of the research involved. You can easily be faced by two children from the same school class, one of whom wants to do a project on dinosaurs and the other on fourteenth-century Byzantine art, where the teacher appears to have given no thought whatever to the possibility that these might not represent tasks of equal difficulty. In these circumstances, you clearly need to get the dinosaur child started quickly, and devote the bulk of your attention to the Byzantine one. The same problems can apply to retirement hobbies, where people have the habit of devoting their declining years to researching the most esoteric topics (frequently family histories) about which the available information is spread very thinly indeed. Either way, the moral for you is clear – you must be able to work out, quickly, what are the most appropriate sources for the job.

Working out the level of specialism

Exactly the same principles apply in working out the level of specialism your enquirer needs. You need both to probe and funnel to find out whether they are looking for information at postgraduate level or are starting from a position of total ignorance. You can use the same sort of questioning strategy as you did above when finding out the level of detail required, but you also have to be both tactful and suspicious. No-one wants to be thought ignorant, and it's only human nature for people to pretend to greater knowledge than they actually have. So you must use the answers to your Who? What? When? Where? Why? How? questions to judge how much your enquirer knows already. Again, this determines the types of source you use – a layperson asking about varicose veins wants *Black's medical dictionary*, but a student doctor probably wants *Lancet*.

There are different *types* as well as *levels* of specialism. An academic and a practitioner might be equally well qualified in their subject. But the academic, about to embark on a piece of original and mould-breaking research, may genuinely need to be aware of everything that has been written about a subject. A practitioner, on the other hand, whose job is to seek a solution to a practical problem, might be perfectly satisfied with just enough information to offer a good spread of options for taking a decision, making a recommendation or taking action. Either way, it is up to you to use your crucial questioning techniques to determine exactly the quantity and quality of information required.

Earmarking and eliminating potential sources

We've actually mentioned a few specific sources in this chapter – *The Times index*, Lexis-Nexis, *Black's medical dictionary*. In reality, though, we haven't reached the sources stage yet. All we've done so far is to discover the subject required, how much information our enquirer wants, and at what level of detail. You may not have a clue yet what actual sources are available to provide the answer you want. But by now you should be able to start forming a judgment on the *kind* of source that will be most helpful. Equally if not more important, you can now start eliminating sources that are less likely to be useful. Remember – it doesn't even matter if these less helpful sources have some of the information you need. Information overload is going to become more of a problem in the immediate future – not less. So you must have the courage to reject information – something which, it has to be said, information professionals have not always found easy to do in the past.

To recap . . .

➤ Beware of information overload, and be ready to reject both sources and information.

➤ Make sure you find out how much information your enquirer needs for the purposes of their task – too much is as unhelpful as too little.

➤ Find out by tactful questioning what level of specialism is appropriate to your enquirer's needs, bearing in mind that academics and practitioners may have different needs.

➤ Identify the most appropriate types of source for the job, and concentrate on those first.

Now at last you have all the information you need to actually start hunting for the answer. But where exactly? It's all very well imagining your ideal source, but how do you discover whether such a source exists? And how do you decide what to do first? In Chapter 3, we'll look at techniques for getting started on answering your enquiry.

Chapter 3
Help! My mind's gone blank
Techniques for getting started

> **In this chapter you'll find out how to:**
>
> ➤ imagine what the final answer will look like
> ➤ decide what kinds of source will provide that answer
> ➤ start identifying actual sources

Let's go back again to your exams. Do you remember how alarming it was? You'd turn the paper over, look at the questions and struggle to fight down the mounting waves of panic as you realized that you couldn't answer any of them. Within a few seconds, though, you'd start seeing through the actual wording to the topic behind it. 'Oh yes,' you'd say to yourself with relief, 'That's really a question about the Scottish succession, and this is really a question about the League of Nations; I can do those.' Well, exactly the same thing can happen with enquiry answering. You've listened carefully to your enquirer. You've asked sensible questions. You know exactly what they want. Your enquirer is standing there waiting for you to help. And you haven't a clue where to start looking.

Fortunately, there are techniques for dealing with this. All you need is a few seconds' thinking time. You can buy this time with a positive response – something like 'I'm sure I can help; let me just think for a moment where would be the best place to start.' But do you know you can really help? The answer is – yes, always. You may not be able to find the precise answer your enquirer wants. But you can always help.

What will the final answer look like?

One good way to get started is to conjure up a picture in your mind's eye of what the final answer will look like. You don't know yet whether there is a source that will provide that answer, but you do at least know what you're looking for, and that's half the battle. Let's see how it would work with some of the questions that our different types of enquirer posed in Chapter 1. (Thanks to our efficient questioning, of course, we now know what they're really looking for instead of what they first asked.)

I'm looking for migration patterns in Wales
This is a request for information that will track and measure the movements of people. So it's probably going to take the form of statistics. However there could be textual commentary on the figures, and they could also be presented as a graph or a diagrammatic map.

Could you tell me how I can gain an NVQ?
So you're looking for details of an organization that administers or awards NVQs. What you will expect to see on the page is its name, address, telephone number and brief details of what it does, so the enquirer can get in touch with it for further help and advice.

What is Marks & Spencer's current pretax profit?
This is quite straightforward – the information is going to take the form of money figures attached to a company name, either on paper or (because it's a business topic, and timeliness is important) on a screen.

I'm doing a project on the Westminster Aquarium
So we're looking for information on a Victorian building in London – not a first-rank one either, like the Crystal Palace (which our muddled enquirer mentioned). There'll be descriptive text and pictures but, because it's not a particularly important building, you're probably not going to find very much about it in any one place.

Cash for Parliamentary questions . . . Strong & Moral Britain Association . . . neo-fascist organizations . . . funding . . . school governors . . . declarations of interest
Quite a shopping list of different kinds of information here. If the cash for questions affair is a hot topic in current affairs right now, then this could take the form of fast-moving news, perhaps on a screen. For the

association, you need not only neutral information about its activities but (because it's dubious) also something probing and investigative. The school governor information is going to take the form of rules, regulations, codes of practice – that sort of thing.

These are by no means the only forms that final answers to enquiries could take. Other possibilities include technical diagrams, pictures, original historical records, bibliographies, recordings, multimedia presentations, even information supplied by a real person. Once you have used your common sense and a bit of imagination to work out what the answer will look like, then you can start looking for actual sources, secure in the knowledge that you're going for the right kind.

What kinds of sources will do the job?

You're making good progress; you've eliminated a good proportion of the stock of your library or information unit because you know it's not going to help you with this enquiry. You're not thrashing round inefficiently, darting off in whatever direction serendipity takes you. You've remained clear headed and logical and you're well on the way to finding the right answer – even though you still don't know what actual sources exist to help you. So let's go back over these enquiries again, to decide what kinds of sources will provide the answer you now know you need.

I'm looking for migration patterns in Wales
You're looking for **statistics** on the movement of people. The **Census** is the principal source of statistics on people, so that's almost certainly the best place to start. However, if the enquirer wants commentary on these migration patterns, or maps and diagrams that might be worth looking for in a sociology or demographic **textbook** – or possibly in a **periodical** produced by the Census-taking authority.

Could you tell me how I can gain an NVQ?
Some kind of training or qualifications **directory** or **handbook** is going to give this kind of information – but if you can't find one of those, a general directory should at least give you a relevant name and address. It may also lead you to the organization's **website**.

What is Marks & Spencer's current pretax profit?
Big companies like Marks & Spencer publish glossy **annual reports,** and most have corporate **websites,** so those are obvious places to look. Failing that, something that gives information on a lot of companies – such as a company **directory** or **database.** Or perhaps you could use an index or database to search through the business pages of a **newspaper,** looking for news of the company's latest results.

I'm doing a project on the Westminster Aquarium
You're going to need a fairly specialist source – a detailed **textbook** on Victorian architecture, or a specialist **guide** to London's buildings. You're probably going to have to hunt through quite a lot of **indexes** to find anything at all. The whole thing has a distinctly nineteenth century feel to it, so perhaps the enquirer's idea of the *Illustrated London news* is worth following up – if it's got a decent **index.**

Cash for Parliamentary questions . . . Strong & Moral Britain Association . . . neo-fascist organizations . . . funding . . . school governors . . . declarations of interest
There's a lot here, so let's take the sources stage by stage.

For the cash for questions affair, you're going to need a really up-to-date news source – an **online database** would be ideal but may be far too costly. There might be a very briskly updated **newspaper index** that would do. Failing that, though, you may have to scan through actual **newspapers** or – better – begin by scanning through **political weeklies** to establish the dates clearly, and then go back to the newspapers of those days for the full detail. If the story's actually breaking now, it would certainly be worth trying a news **website.**

Basic information on the association might come from a **directory,** but comment on its more dubious activities is more likely to have appeared as investigative journalism in newspaper features or journal articles. Because these may have appeared at any time in the past, you need a source that covers a lot of ground quickly – a general **periodicals index** perhaps or, better still, a **CD-ROM.**

The rules for school governors sound pretty specialist; some kind of **encyclopaedia** of education law might help, but maybe you'll have to refer your enquirer to a specialist education **library**. However, common sense would suggest that there's bound to be a digest of a kind, produced by the government specially for school governors. It's probably free, so why not phone up the relevant **government department** and get hold of a copy? It may even be on the **web**.

Identifying actual sources

So now at last we've reached the really hard part – trying to discover whether any actual sources exist that meet your ideal. This is the really daunting bit (isn't it?) – having to learn hundreds of sources and have their details always at your fingertips, so that you can be ready at all times to come out with an instant diagnosis that always seems so impressive when doctors do it. It's true – there are an awful lot of information sources available, and you can spend an entire career answering enquiries and still be discovering new ones on the day you retire. But reassurance is to hand. First of all, successful enquiry work depends on constant daily practice, so the more you do it, the easier it becomes because you can remember more sources without ever having consciously learned them. (Actually this can be a danger as much as an advantage; if you get too used to going to one particular source, you tend to continue using it even if a more efficient one appears.)

The other reassurance, though, is that you can function perfectly effectively by keeping just a few multi-purpose reference sources in mind. Take a look at the list at the front of this book – **twenty-five multi-purpose reference sources you can't afford to ignore.** Between them, they will get you started on a very high proportion of the enquiries you will encounter. They are only a start, of course, and many information professionals would dispute some of the choices and want to substitute alternative candidates of their own. Nevertheless, what these sources (or others like them) can do is set you on the track of other, more specialized sources that you can't possibly be expected to remember. So the basic principle is to get to know a limited number of your most useful local sources (British ones, in the case of the titles listed here) and bear in mind that there is probably an international equivalent – usually (but not always) American.

Learning some basic sources

There's no great mystery to learning a good range of basic sources. If you're working in a public reference or educational library, it will already be well stocked with sources of this kind, and you can spend some time profitably in the early stages of your new job browsing through some of them to see what they can do for you. Two tips – concentrate first on the ones that are shelved behind the enquiry desk. They will be the ones that your more experienced colleagues have found the most useful over the years. And, secondly, when you are examining and evaluating an unfamiliar source, don't just flick through it at random, but make it do something for you. If it's a directory or a statistical journal, look up a specific organization or figure. If it's an encyclopaedia, follow up all the index references to a subject of your choice. If it's a database, give it a really complex task to perform and see how quickly it responds and how relevant its answers are.

Also behind the enquiry desk you may well find an information file, compiled by the staff – the fruit of years of accumulated collective experience of enquiry answering. Such files can be a goldmine of hard-to-find information, once tracked down never forgotten. It could be a simple card index, or a local database on a PC or a set of bookmarked websites. Whatever form it takes, it will be well worth getting to know in detail, because it will be uniquely tailored to your own organization's information specialities and the kinds of questions its enquirers are in the habit of asking.

But what if you are operating on your own, with sole responsibility for the library or information unit of a specialist organization and no-one to turn to for help? Then you should award yourself an afternoon off, go to your nearest large public reference library armed with the list of sources at the front of this book, and ask to see them. Then use them to find out which periodicals, directories, statistical serials and databases will help you in your work.

To recap . . .

➤ Remember that there are techniques you can learn for stopping your mind from going blank – without having to know any actual sources.

➤ Begin by visualizing the final answer in your mind's eye – a long or short piece of continuous text, a list, table, diagram, picture, map, image on a screen.

➤ Then think what kinds of source will provide this answer – textbooks, journals, statistical serials, directories, databases.

➤ Finally start looking for specific sources, bearing in mind that you will only ever have to learn a small number of multi-purpose reference sources in order to begin tackling most enquiries.

Until comparatively recently, once you'd identified which sources would provide the answer you were home and dry. It was then just a question of looking it up, and handing the answer over. Nowadays, though, life isn't quite so simple. Increasingly, you have a choice not only of source, but also of delivery medium, and you'll also encounter the same information source in several different media – print, magnetic disc, CD-ROM, online. Each medium raises different implications for timeliness, user-friendliness, flexibility, cost. So in Chapter 4, we'll think about the different media you could use, and the advantages and disadvantages that each offers.

Chapter 4
More on choosing sources
How to decide which is the best medium for the job

In this chapter you'll find out how to:

➤ **distinguish between different types of information**
➤ **assess the focus, dynamism and complexity of your enquiries**
➤ **compare the merits of printed sources, portable databases and online services**

Back in the 1970s, when the people currently in charge of library and information services were doing their own professional training, their lecturers used to talk with Messianic glee of a future time when commuters would sit on the train, equipped not with a daily newspaper but with a portable microfiche reader. Absurd as it seems now, it was a fairly respectable theory 30 years ago – and maybe we still haven't learned the lessons it offers. To judge from the newspapers nowadays, you'd think that information retrieval had only just been discovered, and that the only way to do it was by means of computers.

Make no mistake – computers are a vital tool of enquiry work, and they are going to become ever more important as electronic media progressively replace many kinds of printed sources, for reasons of cost if for no other. As initiatives such as the People's Network and the National Grid for Learning roll out, so the web will become an even more important medium. There is a persuasive argument which says that public libraries should cut down on buying books (which cost a fraction in real terms of what they did when the public library service started) and concentrate instead on high capital cost online and CD-ROM sources which individuals can't afford.

The paperless office?

But the fact is that ink on paper is still a uniquely valuable medium, and we should be very cautious about predicting its demise, because forecasts like that almost invariably come to grief. It's not yet convenient to take an online service on a train or read it in the bath (although with the growth in Wireless Application Protocol mobile phones – WAP – it soon may be). But, quite apart from the technical limitations of the medium, it still doesn't compare with the flexibility you can achieve by spreading open publications out on a desk, marking their pages, arranging them in piles. The name chosen for the world's most important computer operating system is very telling. After all, who wants to look at something through a Window when they can handle the real thing?

So, as well as deciding what the information your enquirer needs will look like, you also have to determine certain of its other characteristics before you can decide which medium to use.

Different types of information

Faced with similar information available in a range of different media, you have to take decisions on which medium would be most appropriate for the job in hand. This involves deciding, for example, whether the information is fast-moving or hasn't changed for a long time, and whether it's about a single, straightforward subject or is actually about how one issue impinges on another. Let's look at the various types of information you might encounter, and think about the types of source best able provide it.

Broad-based and comprehensive versus narrow and specific

We've already considered the dangers when an enquirer says 'Get me everything you've got on . . .'. It's very unlikely that they literally mean 'everything'. But sometimes people really do want a broad overview of a subject. They might be gathering background information as a preliminary to a more detailed study, or they may just be wanting to brief themselves for a meeting, interview or short-term project. For **broad-based, comprehensive** information, you could use:

➤an entry in a general encyclopaedia (printed or electronic),
➤a chapter in a textbook,
➤a complete textbook.

But if your enquirer has got beyond that stage, and is delving into a subject for more **narrow and specific** detail, you could try:

➤an entry in a special encyclopaedia (printed or electronic),
➤an index entry in a textbook,
➤a report from a specialist organization (i.e. not a conventional publisher),
➤a periodical article (printed or electronic),
➤a table in a statistical journal (printed or electronic),
➤an entry in a directory (printed or electronic),
➤a database record (portable or online).

Static versus dynamic

Static information is complete – finished. It's a matter of history. That's not to say that new research won't be done into it in the future but, to qualify as static, the subject must have reached a full stop at the time your enquirer asks you about it. Deciding that information is static is a hazardous undertaking. Stonehenge may be thousands of years old, but *History today* magazine might still have carried an article in its latest issue on new archaeological finds that tell us more about its purpose or method of construction. But, assuming that you are certain that the information you are being asked about really *is* static, the types of source you could use include:

➤an encyclopaedia or dictionary (printed or electronic),
➤a textbook,
➤a selection of periodical articles (printed or electronic),
➤a statistical time series (printed or electronic),
➤a directory (printed or electronic),
➤a CD-ROM database.

With **dynamic information,** you can't rely on sources of the type shown above because you can't be certain that they will reflect the latest state of affairs. Nevertheless, there are degrees of dynamism; a weekly source may well be sufficient for keeping up to date with medical research, papers for which are frequently submitted months before publication. Stock market prices, on the other hand, can change second by second. Bearing in mind these variations, the kinds of source you could use for dynamic information include:

➤ current newspapers,
➤ recent periodicals,
➤ latest statistical journals,
➤ press releases,
➤ online databases (historical or real-time),
➤ web-based news services,
➤ teletext (broadcast screen-based current information),
➤ audiotex (constantly updated telephone recordings).

One thing you may well find yourself having to do with dynamic information is **browsing and scanning.** There may just not be a sufficiently up-to-date index or searchable database for your purposes; or, if there is, you may not be able to afford to use it. So you might have no alternative but to read quickly through quite a lot of text – a selection of newspaper stories, perhaps, or a set of database records. (We'll look at rapid reading techniques in Chapter 5.)

Single-issue versus multi-faceted

Single-issue enquiries can almost always be summed up in a word or two or a short phrase – 'shopping centres' or 'town planning law'. That doesn't necessarily mean, however, that information on them is going to be easy to find. You might be looking for rare occurrences of a single word or phrase buried in a mass of text. Nevertheless, for single-issue enquiries you might use:

➤ printed sources (if easy to find),
➤ searchable CD-ROMs, or specialist online databases, or the web (if hard to find).

Multi-faceted subjects, on the other hand, are concerned with the impact of one issue upon another – something like 'the planning law implications of non-retail uses of shops in conservation areas'. Fully searchable databases are ideal for multi-faceted subjects; their strength lies in their ability to make and break connections between disparate subjects almost instantaneously. Beware, however – not all databases can do this; web-based news services are built for speed of updating, not searchability, and web search tools don't usually allow you to build searches progressively, in the way you can with professional online services like Lexis-Nexis. So before you decide to use a database to answer a multi-faceted enquiry, make sure that it really *is* fully searchable. However, your chosen database could be a:

➤ portable database – e.g. on a CD-ROM or floppy disk – (if the information is static), or a
➤ specialist online database or the web (if it's dynamic).

(There are two more types of information we need to consider in this context – information that is not available in-house, and information that is not in a published source at all. We'll return to these in Chapter 7.)

Focus, dynamism, complexity

So how do these assessments work on the enquiries that our seven enquirers posed in Chapter 1? Let's quickly review them for their focus, dynamism and complexity.

I'm looking for information on migration patterns in Wales
Focus: Narrow and specific; the enquirer wants one type of population data only.
Dynamism: Relatively static; censuses tend to be taken only once every 10 years, albeit with more frequent intermediate population estimates.
Complexity: Fairly multi-faceted – although this is a standard census enquiry, it does involve combinations and permutations of people and places.
Verdict: Only one source will really do – the Census; since it's designed to answer precisely this kind of enquiry, the printed version will proba-

bly be sufficient, although the CD-ROM version might allow even smaller movements to be identified.

Could you tell me how I can gain an NVQ?
Focus: Narrow and specific; but the range of possible sources where it might be found is still quite wide.
Dynamism: Relatively static, but NVQs are a comparatively recent innovation, and the relevant body might have changed its address several times.
Complexity: Single-issue; once you have identified and located the relevant organization, all further information should be available from there.
Verdict: A recent specialist directory should do; failing that a general directory that will identify and locate the organization for further information. The organization will probably have a website too.

Do you have the electoral register?
Focus: Narrow and specific; only one source will do, but you still don't know whether the enquirer wants the local current register; s/he might need one of 10 years ago from the other end of the country.
Dynamism: Relatively static; electoral registers are revised once a year, but you need to beware of changes around the time the new one is due to appear – and you still don't know whether your enquirer wants the current local register or not.
Complexity: Single-issue, if your enquirer simply wants to check the names at a particular address; but if s/he wants to use it for analytical or market-research purposes, then the official printed version won't really help.
Verdict: Only one source will do, but you need more information before you can hand it over with confidence.

What is Marks & Spencer's current pretax profit?
Focus: Narrow and specific, but the range of sources in which you could find this information remains wide.
Dynamism: Could be very dynamic; the announcement might only have come this morning, or might have been available for months.

Complexity: Single-issue; it's a common, readily available figure.
Verdict: Plenty of sources will give the answer – directories, newspapers and journals, databases, the company's website; but you need to establish first when the figure came out before deciding which medium to go for.

I need earnings data for female employees in Croydon
Focus: Narrow and specific; although our know-all did originally demand the wrong source, at least the enquiry is precisely defined.
Dynamism: Fairly static; it's updated on the basis of an annual sample.
Complexity: Multi-faceted but, like the Census data above, this happens to be a multi-faceted approach that the printed publication can accommodate.
Verdict: There's really only one source that will provide this level of detail on earnings and, at the time of writing, it's only widely available in printed form; when, as is likely, it becomes available as a CD-ROM or on the web, that medium might be worth considering for its possible greater flexibility and ability to manipulate the figures.

I'm doing a project on the Westminster Aquarium
Focus: Narrow and specific – once you have discovered what your muddled enquirer really wants.
Dynamism: Static; this Victorian building was pulled down years ago, and was never of the first rank anyway.
Complexity: Single-issue, although information on it is going to be fairly thinly spread among a lot of sources.
Verdict: Not going to be easy to find; you'll have to skim rapidly through the indexes and contents pages of a lot of books – maybe check on the web too using a search tool (we'll look at these in Chapter 5); however, your muddled enquirer might at least have inadvertently given you a lot of ingenious places to try – books on Victorian architecture, fish displays, the *Illustrated London news*.

Cash for Parliamentary questions . . . Strong & Moral Britain Association . . . neo-fascist organizations . . . funding . . . school governors . . . declarations of interest
Focus: Broad-based and comprehensive? Not really; it's actually a whole range of narrow and specific enquiries.

Dynamism: Pretty dynamic, although variably so; the cash for questions issue could be changing from day to day; with the Association it's difficult to say without checking – the possible neo-fascist connection could be a current issue or might not have been covered for years; rules on school governors are probably subject to fairly regular review to keep up with education policy.

Complexity: Multi-faceted throughout; the press might have handled the cash-for-questions affair in any number of different ways and probably only a searchable database will find them, although if it's very current and your enquirer is sure of the dates, you could scan through current newspapers and journals (using some of the rapid-reading techniques outlined in Chapter 5) or use a newspaper website; you might well need a searchable database too to establish any neo-fascist connections with the association and to locate information on its funding; and finding general information on schools governors' duties and obligations might be fairly straightforward, but what the enquirer has actually asked for is very specific information on declarations of interest.

Verdict: This difficult and sensitive enquiry will need a wide range of sources – searchable databases, news sources, directories, the web perhaps, and probably discreet contact with government officials; it's going to be time-consuming too. (We'll look at deadlines in Chapter 6.)

By the way, did you notice something? Look back at the Focus category in these seven examples; they're all 'Narrow and specific'. That's how it is in real life; even if an enquirer asks a very broad question, and you decide ultimately to use broad-based sources such as general encyclopaedias or textbooks, s/he will always have a reason for asking, and it is on that you must concentrate.

Print, portable databases, online

We've touched on a whole range of media in this chapter, so let's conclude by reviewing the advantages and disadvantages of each.

➤ **Printed sources** are easy to handle, user-friendly and carry no running costs, so you can hand them over to an enquirer with the minimum of initial help. But they can also be out of date, slow to use if you are hunting for information buried in the text, and inflexible if their indexing doesn't accommodate the approach the enquirer wants to take.

➤ **Portable databases**, on CD-ROMs or, less frequently, magnetic disks, can get you to the information fast and can allow for a wide range of approaches to the subject, usually with no running costs. But, although in Windows versions they can be quite easy to use, they do not have the uniform 'look and feel' that a web browser offers, and enquirers might be apprehensive about using them and want you to hold their hand; also, although such sources can be fairly up to date, their carrying capacity is limited, and they can still leave you with the nagging fear that, if you had opted to go online, you might have found much more.

➤ **Online services** can be right up to date, as well as being fast and flexible. But you'll need to take a decision on whether to go for a high cost commercial online service, where accuracy and searching flexibility can be guaranteed, or for free websites, where you might be swamped with poor quality information.

To recap . . .

➤ **Distinguish between broad-based and narrow, static and dynamic, single issue and multi-faceted enquiries.**

➤ **Bear in mind the types of source best suited to the focus, dynamism and complexity of each enquiry.**

➤ **Remember the relative merits of printed sources, portable databases and online services.**

Now that we know exactly which sources we're going to use, we can actually get down to looking things up. In Chapter 5, we'll think about strategies for systematic and efficient searching.

Chapter 5
Do I really know what I'm looking for?
Tips for efficient search strategies

In this chapter you'll find out how to:

➤ **decide what order to try the sources in**
➤ **search systematically**
➤ **change tack if necessary**
➤ **getting the best out of the web**
➤ **employ rapid reading techniques**

We've spent the last four chapters negotiating a labyrinthine and treacherous maze populated by enquirers who don't know or won't tell you what they want, can't speak the language or know too much for their own good. Faced with agonizing decisions on which turnings to take, we've drawn up a careful map of sources which will stop us going round in circles, pick out the main route and skillfully avoid the dead ends. So are we finally out of the maze? No chance! We're right in the middle. To get out again, triumphantly bearing the answer, we've got to go through the whole process once more, in reverse.

Why? Because the pitfalls we will encounter while actually doing the searching are exactly the same as the ones we faced when trying to find out what our enquirers wanted in the first place. This time, however, we'll be pitted against indexes that lead you to the right word but the wrong subject, 'see also' references that take you on a circular tour, and databases that resolutely refuse to tell you anything at all. You don't believe it? Wait and see.

Where to search first

First of all, you have to decide which of the sources you've identified as likely candidates to try first. Once again, this will depend on decisions you've already taken on the subject, the level of detail and specialism, and the currency and complexity of the subject. Possible options are:

> the most **up-to-date** source
> the one most **relevant** to the subject
> the one most **appropriate** to the task in hand.

Let's see how this might work in practice. We'll have a look again at some of our sample enquiries, for which we've now targeted likely sources.

I'm looking for information on migration patterns in Wales
You already know you're going to use the Census to answer this question. It wins on two of the three counts – it's **relevant** (all about population and their movements) and **appropriate** (you're looking for figures). But it's not particularly **up-to-date** (1991) and a vast document, with many specialist volumes. So you'll have to decide whether to go for the migration volume or the Wales volumes first. You're unlikely to have both the printed and CD-ROM versions; but if you do, you need to consider whether the added flexibility and greater level of geographical detail that the CD-ROM might offer justifies the extra skill you'll need to deploy in using it. You'll also have to consider where to look for later estimates of population movements since 1991 (more up to date but less detailed), and whether you need to look for textbooks or periodical articles (just as relevant, perhaps more up to date, but possibly less appropriate because not primarily statistical).

Could you tell me how I can gain an NVQ?
Go for the most **relevant** source first – a specialist education or training directory; this is a fairly open ended enquiry, so the more detail you can find the better, even if you have more **up-to-date** general directories to hand. Only if you can't find a specialist source should you content yourself with brief contact details from a current general directory.

What is Marks & Spencer's current pretax profit?
You should really go for an **up-to-date** source first if you can, since you clearly need to be sure you have the latest figure. The most obvious start-

ing point would be to see if it had a website (we'll look briefly at web searching later in this chapter). Failing that, you may have to consume a lot of time hunting through business periodical indexes or you could try a company directory to begin with; it's a **relevant** and reasonably **appropriate** source, but you must be ready to invest time and/or money in a more up-to-date source if you're not happy with the currency of the figure you find.

I'm doing a project on the Westminster Aquarium
You're going to have to try to find **appropriate** sources here – illustrated books on Victorian architecture or guides to the buildings of London. Being **up-to-date** will be no help at all, and your chances of finding a **relevant** source (a book or article on the Westminster Aquarium itself) are virtually zero.

Cash for Parliamentary questions . . . Strong & Moral Britain Association . . . neo-fascist organizations . . . funding . . . school governors . . . declarations of interest
Very difficult to decide what to go for here. You probably need to be **up to date** for the cash-for-questions aspect, since the story may still be developing – so use an online news service or scan through the papers themselves. For the Association a searchable database or the web seem the most **appropriate** starting point, since you will need to test speculations about funding and links with neo-fascist organizations; you could save money by starting with a less **up-to-date** CD-ROM, but may have to shift to an online source if the information on the CD-ROM is not of recent date. For the guidance for school governors, the school itself would seem the most **relevant** place to go, but it's hardly **appropriate** since your enquirer doesn't want to alert the school; the more remote Department for Education & Employment is equally **relevant**, and far more **appropriate**.

Searching systematically

Now you've finally decided on your first source, what are you going to search for? Plenty of things can go wrong, and you have to be ready for them. It's all really a matter of common sense, but you must spend a few moments thinking out your strategy. Among the myriad things that can cause problems, these are some that you should certainly consider.

Synonymous, broader, narrower and related terms

Really well-constructed indexes are based on a thesaurus which allows for all the different approaches that a searcher could take towards a subject. Alas, however, the real world is full of ineptly constructed indexes. So it's wise to assume that you will have to fend for yourself. Whether you're using a printed index or a free-text database, take a little time before you start searching to scribble down your own mini structured thesaurus. It will minimize your chances of missing something relevant and – just as important – it will help you to avoid wasting your time by accidentally going over the same ground twice. Suppose you've been asked for information about railway management. You might write down:

➤ rail services, train services (synonymous terms)
➤ public transport, surface transport, fixed links (broader terms)
➤ commuting, rapid transit (narrower terms).

Once you've been through this little exercise, stick to it when searching and you'll be sure you're making the most efficient use of your time (but see 'Changing tack' below).

Variant spellings

Whether you're using a conventional index or a database, variant spellings can cause big problems, so try to anticipate them. Proper names are especially tricky; it was Cain who killed Abel, but Kane who had a sled called *Rosebud*. And where on earth do you start looking for the fast food chain that calls itself *Mc*Donalds but calls its culinary *pièce de résistance* a Big *Mac*? Many of the databases, and quite a few of the printed sources, that you use will be American, so you will have to watch out for 'color' instead of 'colour', 'disk' instead of 'disc'. This may not be a great problem with alphabetical indexes; your eye will quickly spot the difference. But, with many databases, you're flying blind, and if you search for 'favourite' or 'labour' they'll keep on giving you a zero result no matter how much you swear at them. There are plenty of other pitfalls with variant spellings in British English – jails can be gaols, choirs can be quires (in more archaic sources anyway) – one could go on but that's enough.

Homonyms

It's extremely frustrating to be looking for hardware suppliers and constantly coming up with farmers in Georgia, but that's what tends to happen with a word like 'nuts', which is equally at home in the two phrases 'nuts & bolts' and 'monkey nuts'. Numismatists studying the indented wax symbols at the base of ancient documents must find it equally annoying when a hunt for 'seals' keeps leading them to Arctic sea mammals. And specialists in literacy keep finding themselves being vexingly directed to a large Berkshire town when they look up 'reading'. You need to be particularly alive to the dangers of homonyms, and be ready with tactics for taking evasive action if necessary. It's particularly – but not exclusively – a problem with free-text database searching (including the web). Strategies that you can employ to deal with it include adding a further qualifying term to your search – such as 'numismatics' or 'literacy' – or, in the case of the 'nuts' problem, using a trade classification code (if one is available) instead of the word.

British versus American usage

Again this is a particular problem with database searching, where American sources still tend to predominate. Most people would probably remember to use 'elevator' instead of 'lift', 'streetcar' instead of 'tram' and 'pants' instead of 'trousers' (although this last one presents its own special homonym problems as well). But how many Europeans know that the American for 'central heating' is 'space heating', and is equally unfindable whether you are using a database or a printed index.

Changing tack

But it's when things start to go wrong that your careful preparation for searching, as outlined in the section on 'Searching systematically' above will really start to pay off. Hunting for information is a journey into the unknown. Every source you use will be differently constructed, and have its own indexing quirks. As your searching progresses, it's almost inevitable that you will come across relevant words and phrases that you never thought of in the first place, and that's when you'll have to take the difficult decision on whether it's worth going back over sources that you've looked at already.

If you do, your mini-thesaurus should at least help to ensure that you don't merely repeat work that you've already done. Let's go back to those train services; suppose you're onto your fourth possible source, and you suddenly find the following entries:

➤ Commuting *see* Suburban rail services
➤ Rapid transit *see also* Light rail

These entries show two further terms which, in an ideal world, you would have thought of for yourself when you constructed your mini-thesaurus. This 'See' reference should mean that there are *no index entries at all* under 'Commuting' (the term you first searched on), and that *all* the entries are under 'Suburban rail services' (the indexer's preferred term). With the 'See also' reference, on the other hand, there could be relevant entries under *either* 'Rapid transit' *or* 'Light rail' because, for the purposes of this index, they're similar but not identical.

These discoveries should prompt you to do two things. Firstly, you must amend your mini-thesaurus, as follows:

➤ Rail services, train services (synonymous terms)
➤ Public transport, surface transport, fixed links (broader terms)
➤ Commuting, rapid transit, *suburban rail services* (narrower terms)
➤ *Light rail* (related term)

Secondly you must decide whether or not to go back over previous sources and recheck for the new terms. If you do decide to do this, all you should have to do is check under the newly discovered terms. If there's nothing extra to be found under them, then you should be able to abandon the source without wasting any more time on it. (We'll discuss efficient management of your time in Chapter 6.)

Searching databases efficiently

Printed indexes will use 'See' and 'See also' references with varying degrees of efficiency and consistency. Databases, on the other hand, can offer a whole range of further searching aids. They may be able to display an alphabetical list of the words and phrases adjacent to the one you've chosen. They might be based on a structured thesaurus, which you can actually call up on screen and examine for possible further search terms. They may employ a hierarchical numeric classification which will automatically retrieve all records classified below the point at which you actually enter. They'll almost certainly allow you to use truncation, so that a search on the term 'rail*' can automatically retrieve 'railway' and 'railroad' (and 'railings', so beware!). More sophisticated searching software may also offer relevance ranking, or even natural language searching in which the software can actually interpret a phrase like 'Travelling in to work by train'. Whatever help is at your disposal you must be ready to modify your searching strategy in the light of information retrieved – and to do so systematically.

Getting the best out of the web

The enquiry answering capabilities of the world wide web have improved beyond all recognition over the years; it's still not going to be the answer to everything, but it is now nevertheless an essential enquiry answering tool.

Most of our seven enquiries would be worth a try on the web at some stage. Almost all major institutions, and very many tiny ones, have promotional websites, so the web is particularly good at providing background information on named organizations and initiatives – worth trying for the NVQ and Marks & Spencer enquiries. It is also a natural home for pressure groups, so an anti-racist organization's site may well yield useful cautionary information about the Strong & Moral Britain Association. It's a great place for enthusiasts to pursue their individual obsessions too, so a quick speculative search for material on the Westminster Aquarium might pay dividends. But do make sure that you are quick; web pages are littered with tempting links to other sites, and if you are induced to follow any, make sure you don't forget what you enquirer's question was in the first place. Bear in mind, too, that there's little if any quality control over many websites, so there's no guarantee that what you find will be authoritative or accurate.

Searching with a purpose

Speculative searching probably means using search tools. These index the contents of the millions of web pages available and usually attempt to rank them for relevance. Your web browser will have a button offering links to some of them, and so probably will your Internet service provider's home page. You'll discover others by yourself as well. Some of the best known ones are:

➤ AltaVista (**http://www.altavista.com**)
➤ Excite (**http://www.excite.com**)
➤ Google (**http://www.google.com**)
➤ HotBot (**http://www.hotbot.com**)
➤ InfoSeek (**http://www.infoseek.com**)
➤ Lycos (**http://www.lycos.com**)
➤ Northern Light (**http://www.northernlight.com**)
➤ Webcrawler (**http://www.webcrawler.com**)

In addition, there are several 'meta' search services, which search the other search tools. They tend to bring back only limited numbers of results, which can save you having to wade through screenfuls of hits, but they don't necessarily allow you to take advantage of the individual search tools' special characteristics. The best known ones are:

➤ Ask Jeeves (**http://www.askjeeves.com**)
➤ Dogpile (**http://www.dogpile.com**)
➤ Metacrawler (**http://www.metacrawler.com**)

A growing number of search tools have UK or other country equivalents – you'll be able to link to these from their main sites, or you could try experimenting by substituting .co.uk for .com. Some have 'power search' facilities, allowing you to use slightly more sophisticated search techniques and hopefully achieve more precise results. HotBot has a special 'find people' feature and another service, Deja.com, specializes in searching newsgroups – cooperative sites to which people with some common interest contribute. Finally, Yahoo! is a rather special case. It's not strictly a search tool so much as a detailed classification of websites with different versions for each country. You can find it at:

➤ http://www.yahoo.com
➤ http://www.yahoo.co.uk

. . . and so on for other countries. Of all these search tools, my favourite are Google and Metacrawler. They both usually returns a manageable number of hits and do well at producing relevant results. There's no reason why these need be your favourites, though. So experiment with them all, ask your colleagues' opinion, and reach your own conclusions.

Even though they each index only a fraction of the web's total content, search tools do still tend to produce vast numbers of hits, and it's not always obvious why some items have been retrieved at all. So it's often more efficient to start with a search tool, but then to follow links as soon as you get to a nearly relevant site. For example, a search on National Vocational Qualifications might lead you initially to the website of an institution that promotes its own NVQ courses, but which also includes link to official information on NVQs in general. Another way is to find an organization's web address in a conventional printed source – a directory or an advert for example – and then go online for further details.

Web addresses – have a guess

If you can't find an organization's web address, you can always try guessing it. It doesn't work every time of course, but it's surprising how often it does, with practice. It would certainly be worth trying this technique to see if Marks & Spencer has a site that gives its pretax profit. Some possible guesses might be:

➤ http://www.marks&spencer.com
➤ http://www.m&s.co.uk

➤ http://www.marks-and-spencer.com
➤ http://www.marks_and_spencer.co.uk

If you do guess, you also need to know what domain to try – the bit that indicates the type of organization. These are some of the commonest:

➤ .com (global commercial sites)
➤ .ac or .edu (educational institutions)
➤ .co (single country commercial sites)
➤ .gov (government departments and agencies)
➤ .org (associations, professional bodies, organizations)

Finally, you'll need the country code. United States sites don't usually have a country code at all, British sites have .uk and it's not too difficult to work out the rest. Here are a few examples.

➤ .au (Australia)
➤ .ca (Canada)
➤ .be (Belgium)
➤ .ch (Switzerland)
➤ .de (Germany)
➤ .fr (France)
➤ .nl (Holland)

igh quality information

More and more high quality information is becoming available free on the web, including the whole of *Encyclopaedia Britannica* (**http://www.britannica.com**), news and topical features from the BBC (**http://www.bbc.co.uk**) and business information from the *Financial Times* (**http://www.ft.com** – probably one of the best known web addresses in the world). Government puts lots of information online too; try looking at **http://www.open.gov.uk** (good on government departments or agencies and their functions), or **http://www.ukstate.com** (for citizenship information such as house purchase, divorce, learning to drive, business regulations or government services). As you can see, this last example is actually a commercial site, run by the privatized Stationery Office, and like many of this kind, the free information is a taster to tempt you to buy commercial services.

The Welsh migration and Croydon earnings queries might be worth trying on the web; take a look at the Office of National Statistics' Statbase site, for example (**http://www.statistics.gov.uk**). However most statistical information from government tends to be current data from press releases rather than retrospective time series, so in this instance the web may do little more than throw up suggestions for sources or contacts.

Although anyone can use the web with very little introduction, it takes skill to use it well. It's now such a fundamental tool for enquiry answering that it's worth taking some time out to learn how to use it properly. Library Association Publishing publishes several titles on Internet use – not just the web, which is merely the multimedia part of the Net. You'll find details of *The library and information professional's guide to the Internet* and *A guide to finding quality information on the Internet* in the bibliography.

Finally, don't forget to bookmark the useful sites you find – either temporarily for the purposes of the current enquiry, or permanently as part of your library's useful information file. Be disciplined about arranging your bookmarks logically too. There's nothing more frustrating than not being able to find the wonderful site you were using only yesterday.

Rapid reading

You can't always rely on printed sources having an index. And, even if there is a suitable online database for your purposes, you may not be able to afford to use it. So there will be times when you find yourself having to scan and browse rapidly through the text of an actual document or web page. You might find yourself having to look at a selection of newspaper stories, a set of on-screen headlines, or a chapter of an inadequately indexed book. If this happens, you certainly don't have to read every word. There are techniques that you can learn for rapid and efficient reading, and it's a good idea to practise them. Some of the commonest ones are:

➤ reading down the middle of the page (or screen), relying on your peripheral vision to spot significant words
➤ looking for capitalized words (e.g. the names of organizations), abbreviations and numerals
➤ looking at bullet points or lists first
➤ deciding what unusual words are peculiar to your enquiry, and concentrating on spotting those
➤ reading the first sentence of each paragraph.

Rapid reading techniques only work if you already have a clear idea of what you're looking for. Your eye won't instinctively spot a significant word or phrase unless you've already worked out what those words or phrases are. So constructing your own mini-thesaurus is just as important for browsing and scanning as it is for using indexes.

To recap . . .

➤ Decide whether to go for the most up-to-date, most relevant or most appropriate source first.
➤ Construct your own mini-thesaurus before you start searching.
➤ Beware of variant spellings, homonyms, and British versus American usage.
➤ Be ready to change your search strategy (and amend your mini-thesaurus) in the light of what you find.
➤ Exploit the web – using search tools, following links, guessing web addresses.
➤ Learn and practise rapid reading techniques for scanning and browsing.

All of this takes time, and you start out with no guarantee of success. So what do you do when you realize that time is running out and you're no nearer an answer than you were when you started? In Chapter 6, we'll look briefly at efficient time management, which allows you to meet deadlines every time.

Chapter 6
Quick! Time's running out
How to meet deadlines every time

In this chapter you'll find out how to:

➤ **distinguish between vital and urgent tasks**
➤ **establish a working timetable**
➤ **compromise on the answer**
➤ **provide progress reports**

Internet ads have a lot to answer for. How many times have you seen or heard phrases like 'A world of information at your fingertips'? The trouble is that enquirers believe them. They really do think that their friendly reference librarian or information officer can produce anything they want with a few deft mouse clicks. The web, they think, has it all. You can't really blame them. Internet service providers, portal operators and – it has to be said – incautiously upbeat librarians have all raised their expectations to the point where, as far as they're concerned, the information superhighway is complete down to the last white line.

Fax and e-mail haven't helped either. A decade ago, dealing with written enquiries did at least give you a breathing space, in which you could agree a realistic deadline that allowed you to work out a sensible search strategy including provision for things going wrong. Nowadays, though, enquirers know that they can have a written answer instantly; blaming delays on the post is no longer an option. Now increasingly widespread use of e-mail is encouraging enquirers to demand even tighter deadlines.

So what can you do about it? The first thing is to maintain a positive attitude, keep a clear head, and distinguish between what's vital and what's urgent.

Vital versus urgent

We discovered in Chapter 1 that 'urgent' is not an acceptable deadline for any enquiry. You need to know *how* urgent; you need a date and/or a time. Now we need to take that a stage further and make sure that we really understand what we mean by urgency.

Faced with a limited amount of time and a number of competing tasks, you need first of all to sort them into priority order and allocate time between them – and you need to revise that timetable constantly as new tasks come along to demand your attention. To do this, you need to be clear about the relative importance and difficulty of the tasks before you. Let's deal with importance first. A 'vital' task is one without which your organization cannot function. An 'urgent' task is one which has an imminent deadline; it may or may not be vital. If you don't buy information sources, catalogue and index them and learn how they work, then you can't answer the enquiries. So these are 'vital' tasks. But they're not necessarily 'urgent'; if you put them off until tomorrow, no great harm may be done. They may in due course become urgent; if you're constantly being asked for information that's sitting in a document that you haven't yet catalogued, or a CD-ROM that you haven't yet installed, then that cataloguing or installation becomes not only 'vital' but also 'urgent'. Let's see how it might apply to enquiry work.

First come first served?

You might have three urgent enquiries to do. They all have the same deadline. But one is for an important client, another is for your managing director, and the third is for a colleague doing a college course on day release. Your job is to answer enquiries for all these three people, so they're all vital; if you don't do them, you'll be in trouble. But if you fail your colleague you'll probably just get ticked off; if you fail the managing director you might lose your job, and if you fail the client, everyone might lose their jobs. So you can see that there are degrees of urgency, depending on how vital the task is. You might deal with it by:

➤**firstly** suggesting an appropriate source for the colleague to use for him or herself

51

➤**secondly** warning the managing director that you're doing an enquiry for an important client and either providing a brief 'holding' answer for the MD or negotiating a longer deadline (or both), and then

➤**thirdly** concentrating on the client.

Once you've dealt with your competing enquiries in the manner outlined above, you can then work out how long you need to allocate to each. Five minutes with the library catalogue may be enough for your college colleague, and 15 minutes looking up and photocopying or downloading a few pieces of information will put the MD on the back-burner for a while. This leaves you the rest of the morning to spend doing database searches, scanning journal references and compiling a list of addresses for the client. (And preparing to present the answer in a helpful way; we'll look at adding value in Chapter 8.)

Of course, it doesn't work like this in a busy reference or educational library. There every enquirer is equally important, and you have to employ different techniques to ensure that everyone's deadlines are met. To do this, you really need to be able to assess instantly the relative difficulty of answering each enquiry. There's probably no easy way of doing this; it comes with experience and, even then, you will still come across enquiries that turn out to be almost impossible to answer, even though you thought they would be easy. But you can help yourself by making sure that you know your basic reference sources really well – just a strictly limited number of them, such as the ones listed at the front of this book. If you are familiar with their contents, then you will know what's feasible and where you're going to have to negotiate with the enquirer about providing a compromise answer.

Time is money

Difficulty doesn't necessarily equate to time (although it might). An alternative to spending time on a difficult enquiry might be to use a database, where the time saved justifies the expense. Assuming that you've correctly identified the right one to use, searchable databases can save you an enormous amount of time – not least because they *fail* as quickly as they *succeed*. Just think about it for a moment. If you use printed sources, it takes you longer to fail to find the answer than it does to succeed because, once you've found it, you stop looking. Whereas if you keep not finding it, you go on looking until you've exhausted every possibility. A database, on the other hand, fails as quickly as it succeeds, so you know much further ahead of the deadline that an enquiry is going to be difficult, and you still have time to do something about it.

The moral here is that time is money. Whether you choose to spend pounds on an online search that takes five minutes, or restrict yourself to 'free' printed sources or the web and spend an hour looking things up or surfing instead, the result is the same – cost to your organization. In making efficient use of your time, and deciding when to call a halt and compromise on the answer instead, you must always bear in mind that every minute you spend on an enquiry is costing your organization money. It's not just the cost of your salary either, or the online or copying charges – there are overheads to take into account as well – things like lighting, heating, rent and rates, to say nothing of the cost of acquiring your library's stock in the first place. The less efficiently you plan your search strategy, the more it costs your organization.

Your working timetable

We've already done some assessment of the relative difficulty of our sample enquiries. Assuming that they all have the same deadline (and that your library or information unit has all the sources necessary for answering them), let's see what this is likely to mean for our timetabling.

I'm looking for information on migration patterns in Wales
Verdict: A very small quantity of looking up in a guide to statistics should tell you that the Census is the place to look. But the Census is a huge document. So this enquiry is fairly **easy** but could be a bit **slow**.

Could you tell me how I can gain an NVQ?
Verdict: You've discovered enough to know that you need specialist training directories, although that may have taken you some little time. So this enquiry will probably turn out to be fairly **easy** but a bit **slow**.

Do you have the electoral register?
Verdict: It will probably take only a minute or two to check that the enquirer wants the current register for the local area, so this enquiry is very **easy**, very **quick**.

What is Marks & Spencer's current pretax profit?
Verdict: This enquiry is **easy** because there are plenty of places where the figure could be found, and could be **quick** if you use the web.

I need earnings data for female employees in Croydon
Verdict: Your enquirer didn't help to start with by suggesting an inappropriate source; but once you've sorted that out, finding the right source should be a simple looking-up job in a statistics sourcebook. So this enquiry will eventually turn out to be **easy** and quite **quick**.

I'm doing a project on the Westminster Aquarium
Verdict: Once you've interpreted this enquirer's muddle, you'll probably find that the answer requires a lot of looking up for not much information. So this one will be **hard** and **slow**.

Cash for Parliamentary questions . . . Strong & Moral Britain Association . . . neo-fascist organizations . . . funding . . . school governors . . . declarations of interest
Verdict: This is a very big job; it's going to involve looking things up, searching databases and phoning round. You might be able to speed some parts of it up by using databases, but there are so many aspects to it, and some of them are so speculative, that it's still going to take a long time. So it's **hard** and **slow**.

Finally, then, let's use these assessments to sort the enquiries into priority order, so that everybody gets started as quickly as possible.

1 *Do you have the electoral register?* (Very easy, very quick.)
2 *What is Marks & Spencer's current pretax profit?* (Easy and probably quick.)
3 *I need earnings data for female employees in Croydon.* (Easy and quite quick.)

4 *I'm looking for information on migration patterns in Wales.* (Fairly easy but could be a bit slow.)

5 *Could you tell me how I can gain an NVQ?* (Fairly easy but could well be slow.)

6 *I'm doing a project on the Westminster Aquarium.* (Hard and slow, but at least you can leave the enquirer browsing.)

7 *Cash for Parliamentary questions . . . Strong & Moral Britain Association . . . neo-Fascist organizations . . . funding . . . school governors . . . declarations of interest.* (Hard and slow, and the enquirer will need a lot of help.)

Beware! This is not the right order for everyone. People's perception of difficulty varies depending on their experience, so you should take this section as a guide to technique, not as the answer to the problem.

If you're actually doing all the enquiries yourself, your chosen order of priority means that you can start getting answers out from the earliest possible moment. If you're simply helping the enquirers to find the answers for themselves, then this strategy means that everyone gets started as rapidly as possible and you have time to monitor everybody's progress and help wherever necessary.

A compromise answer

But, unfortunately, even this can't guarantee success. It may be that you really have more to do than you can possibly manage in the time available. In that case, you may well find yourself having to compromise on the answer. Do avoid ever saying 'no' if you possibly can, but you have to accept that there will be times when you have to say 'yes but . . .'. The important thing is to try to advance on all fronts – leave everybody with something, rather than some with a complete answer and others with nothing. There are various things you can do to keep to your deadlines.

Suggest sources rather than finding answers

This is an obvious tactic, and enquirers are usually sympathetic if they can see that you're under pressure from other people standing round. But it can be harder to convince enquirers that you are short of time if there's no-one else around, no matter how many jobs you are working on for absent enquirers. And don't expect to get any sympathy if you actually list for the enquirer's edification all the other things you have to do – that's your problem, not theirs. If you do have to resort to suggesting sources, make sure that you explain fully to the enquirer how the source works; show them the different indexes available in a printed source, take them through the various menus or buttons on a CD-ROM. And invite them to return for further advice if the source doesn't work; don't ever give the impression that you're fobbing them off.

Suggest alternative libraries or information units

Suggesting sources doesn't work with telephone enquirers. If you can't help them immediately, you could suggest an alternative library or information unit that they could try. But again, be as helpful as possible in doing this. Look up the organization's phone and fax numbers in a directory, and tell your telephone enquirer exactly what it can do that you can't. Beware, too, of directing enquirers to institutions that they are not entitled to use. Some will accept enquiries only from their members or subscribers; others will want to charge.

Ask for thinking time

An equally good tactic when dealing with telephone enquirers is to say 'Leave it with me; I'll see what I can do.' This buys you valuable time and leaves the enquirer satisfied that you are taking the enquiry seriously. Don't forget to agree a deadline, though; and remember that the onus to do this is on you.

Offer a compromise answer

Of course, asking for thinking time merely leaves you with yet another deadline to meet. In that case, an alternative tactic is to offer a compromise answer. (This tactic works equally well whether the enquirer is standing in front of you or has communicated by phone, fax or e-mail.) A compromise answer is usually a briefer one – whatever you can find in a few minutes in readily accessible sources. However there are some occasions when a compromise answer can be a longer one. It might take only a few minutes to do a rough and ready database search and hand the results over unchecked, whereas if you had the time, you might go through the results on your word processor and remove the less relevant material. (This is all part of adding value, and we'll return to it in Chapter 8.)

Progress reports

Whatever strategies you choose to employ to ensure you meet your deadlines, it's always a good idea to keep enquirers informed on how you're getting on. You're likely to do this automatically when the enquirer is standing over you, but you should get into the habit of doing it for absent enquirers too. It's reassuring – what doctors call a good bedside manner – and it shows that you're being open about any difficulties and not trying to pull the wool over your enquirer's eyes. And, although you'll always hope to succeed in finding the answer, progress reports can also prepare enquirers for disappointment (and put them in a mood for accepting a compromise answer) if your searching is going badly. Making progress reports may seem irksome and time-consuming, but it undoubtedly pays public relations dividends.

To recap . . .

➤ **Make sure you understand the difference between vital and urgent tasks.**
➤ **Establish a working timetable, grading and prioritizing enquiries according to whether they are easy or hard, quick or slow.**
➤ **Buy time if necessary by supplying sources instead of doing the searching, or suggesting alternative institutions, or asking for thinking time, or offering a compromise answer.**
➤ **Always keep your enquirers informed about progress.**

All of this assumes, of course, that you actually have some hope of finding the answer. But what do you do if it's nowhere to be found? In Chapter 7, we'll think about what to do if your chosen sources fail to come up with the answer at all.

Chapter 7
Can't find the answer – what now?
What to do if your chosen sources fail

In this chapter you'll find out how to:

➤ **prepare your enquirer for disappointment**
➤ **settle for an alternative answer**
➤ **look for outside help**
➤ **decide whether it's worth buying the information in**

A few years back a big motor accessories supplier ran a national advertising campaign under the slogan 'The answer is "yes" – now what's the question?' It was a bit of a cheat because it presumably only meant questions about vehicle parts. But you can't fault the attitude behind it.

We've already looked at the problem of information overload, in Chapter 2. But it has a positive side as well. It means that the likelihood of failing to find an answer to any enquiry is diminishing all the time. More and more information is available online, and technological developments in typesetting and printing mean that more information than ever can also be published cost-effectively in paper form.

Saying 'no' positively

So is there any excuse for failing to find the answer? Sometimes. Your enquirer may decide that the information is just not worth the cost of going online or using a commercial information broker. You may decide that you can't afford to invest the time on a speculative and possibly fruitless attempt to find a website that might be able to help. So, no matter how much technology you surround yourself with, and no matter how well funded your organization is, you might still have to admit defeat.

But this still doesn't mean saying 'no'. It means exercising ingenuity in helping your enquirer to continue travelling hopefully instead of hitting a cul de sac. It means thinking positively about what you can still do. Remember the technique you used when your mind went blank in Chapter 3? You said 'I'm sure I can help,' and indeed you still can – although by now not necessarily in the way your enquirer expected.

Preparing your enquirer for disappointment

So it's probably just as well to start lowering your enquirer's expectations as soon as you realize there are going to be difficulties. This is where the progress reports mentioned in Chapter 6 come in. You'll be in a much better position to help your enquirer if s/he is already aware that you are having problems and is starting to think about what alternative answers would be acceptable.

What you can do to save the situation at this stage will depend on what exactly your enquirer wants the information for. As we discovered in Chapter 4, people rarely want information merely to satisfy idle curiosity – they nearly always have a purpose in asking. This means that you can sometimes accommodate their needs by providing an alternative answer – less specific than the one they asked for, for example, but almost as helpful in enabling them to reach the conclusion they seek or put forward the argument they want to promote. To decide where to look for this, you need to go back to the technique we looked at in Chapter 3, and try to imagine the appearance not of an ideal answer but of an acceptable alternative.

Where else can you go?

If you don't have anything in-house that might provide the answer, then you can always seek outside help. This offers you lots of scope; there are thousands of sources you could consider, and plenty of places you can look to identify them. But seeking outside help usually imposes delays on the answer and, as we saw in Chapter 6, you frequently don't discover that you're in difficulties until the deadline is looming. So a third possibility is to go online for the information; but this can be expensive, and your enquirer would presumably have to bear the cost.

59

The really important thing at this stage is to keep your enquirer informed. You have to be realistic about it; you are the bearer of bad news, and your job now is to soften its impact. You need further help from your enquirer on what would be an acceptable way of salvaging the enquiry, so you need to go right back to the kinds of questions and answers that we looked at in Chapter 1 – almost a repeat of the original dialogue, but with a changed agenda.

Of course, you might have anticipated the difficulties, using the easy/hard and quick/slow assessments that we looked at in Chapter 6. And you will of course have decided (as we discussed in Chapter 4) whether to go for the most up to date, most relevant or most appropriate sources first. So you may well be quite clear what your next move must be, without any further reference to your enquirer. But warn them, nevertheless.

Looking for outside help

There are hundreds of possible sources that can lead you to outside help on every conceivable topic, and you will be very unlucky indeed if you can't find anywhere at all to direct your enquirer to. (Have another look at the 25 multi-purpose reference sources at the front of this book; *most* of them can lead you to further sources of help.) Seeking outside help also has the advantage of sticking to the enquirer's agenda, whereas if you suggest a substitute answer, you inevitably shift the agenda to suit you. But going outside does introduce a further delay, and it also means that you can no longer necessarily guarantee the attention and courtesy that you are of course giving your own enquirer. Remember, an unsatisfactory response from a source that you have recommended can rebound on you.

The NVQ enquiry is an ideal candidate for outside help. From your own researches in education and training directories, you will have discovered that the initials stand for National Vocational Qualifications, and you will have located the National Council for Vocational Qualifications as the relevant authority. You'll have its address, phone, fax and e-mail, a brief description of its responsibilities and activities, and common sense will tell you that if you or your enquirer give them a call, they'll undoubtedly be able to provide further literature on getting started with an NVQ. This is just about the simplest and most straight-forward referral you can do.

But it's not the only kind of referral you can do. You might draw a complete blank with the Strong & Moral Britain Association. If it's the kind of organization your enquirer suspects, with neo-Fascist connections, then it might not be particularly forthcoming with information about itself for publication in directories. So that's when you might need to exercise a bit of imagination and think what kinds of alternative sources would be interested in helping. Anti-racist organizations seem the obvious candidates; a quick check of a source like the *Directory of British associations* would reveal the Institute of Race Relations and the National Association of Community Relations Councils as two possible candidates, and would tell you whether either had a library or offered an information service.

You can actually use the web to ask other libraries for help. *Ask a Librarian* is a splendid cooperative venture involving a number of public library services whose staff undertake to answer enquiries from the public by e-mail within two working days (**http://www.earl.org.uk/ask/index. html**). Be very careful not to abuse such a service, though. Remember, enquiry answering is your job and there's no excuse for becoming lazy!

Asking authors

You can use the results of your literature searching for a third type of referral – to the authors of nearly relevant books or articles, or the editors of what seem like appropriate periodicals. Your hunt for material on the Westminster Aquarium may have led you to a lovely coffee-table book on Victorian pleasure palaces, with just one picture of the Aquarium and a brief caption. So why not try contacting the author? You might find him or her in one of a number of *Who's who*-type publications that cover writers, but sources of this kind are always highly selective in who they include, and are not always particularly up-to-date; so an alternative would be to use the book's publisher as a go-between. Actually this isn't an ideal solution either, because professional authors (as opposed to enthusiasts) are often reluctant to enter into correspondence, and publishers tend to be protective of their authors too. A better alternative might be to scrutinize the bibliography to see if it can lead you to more detailed literature that your enquirer might be able to see in a specialist library, or borrow through the British Library Document Supply Centre.

Contacting authors of articles in specialist periodicals, or the editors of those periodicals, can be more fruitful. With a radical agenda to pursue, they may be more committed to their subject than a jobbing author or commercial book publisher would be. So the editor of *NAGM news* (the journal of the National Association of Governors and Managers, which you've identified through *Willing's press guide* or *Benn's media*) might be prepared to advise on issues of conflicts of interest for school governors, or even (for a price) provide an off-print of a recent article.

Buying the information in

When you've exhausted all these possibilities, there may be no alternative to buying the information in. You could use directories of information brokers to identify people or institutions that could actually take the enquiry off your hands and do it for you. You'd not only be buying time that you were not able to devote to the enquiry yourself, but probably also some kind of expertise in the subject concerned. If the labour market data in the *New earnings survey* turned out to be insufficient for your enquirer about female earnings in Croydon, then you could go to a broker who specialized in locating and supplying statistical data and who had access to the National Online Manpower Information Service (NOMIS) or to data from independent pay consultants such as Incomes Data Services.

But this can be hugely expensive; you'd be paying every penny of the broker's costs, plus their profit. Costly as it may seem in cash terms, using a commercial online database would almost certainly work out cheaper (assuming, that is, you were a reasonably efficient searcher who worked out their strategy beforehand and didn't waste ages wondering what to do next while actually connected on a pay-as-you-go basis). An extensive full text periodical article service, such as Lexis-Nexis, may be essential for information on the Strong & Moral Britain Association.

Expensive online?

In real terms, online services are actually becoming cheaper. This is partly because of technological developments, which mean that the prices charged by the existing commercial services have risen by less than the rate of inflation, but also because of the introduction of new pricing packages. Fixed price services for business, such as FT Discovery or Profound, would provide an instant up-to-date answer on Marks & Spencer's current pretax profit because that's what they are designed to do. But although they are fixed price (or nearly so), that price is high – several thousand pounds a year – and probably only a specialist business information library would regard the cost as justified.

Settling for an alternative answer

After you've reviewed all these other options, there's probably nothing else left now but to suggest an alternative answer. Let's have a think about possible substitute answers to a couple of our sample enquiries. You might not have full migration figures for Wales from the Census, because you only have a limited selection of official statistics. But a good statistics sourcebook should have led you to *Regional trends*, an annual digest that includes some population figures for Wales and its surrounding English regions including one short table of net migration figures. Would this be acceptable? That would be for your enquirer to decide.

The Westminster Aquarium enquiry is likely to prove particularly frustrating. It will probably take you ages to pull together a pathetic little selection of references. If you've managed a brief entry in an encyclopaedia of London, an illustration from a book of Victorian views and a few sentences gleaned from the indexes of textbooks, then you'll have done very well indeed. But remember that your enquirer is doing a project – for school or college, one assumes. S/he needs enough material for a 500-word essay, so what can you add? Why not suggest broadening the scope of the project to take in other popular Victorian entertainment venues in London, or social studies on the growth of working-class wealth and leisure during the nineteenth century? There should be plenty of material on both these topics – indeed, you'll already be in a position to recommend suitable sources, because you'll have come across them while actually looking for references to the Aquarium. Your hapless enquirer, whose own deadline will undoubtedly be tight (students only seem to come to the library for help at the last moment) will probably fall upon you with gratitude. But beware! You've changed the agenda in this enquiry to suit yourself; so be especially sensitive to your enquirer's reaction, to make sure that the suggested change also suits them. Your enquirer will not be impressed if you try to present an alternative answer as a lovely surprise.

To recap . . .

➤ **Keep your enquirer informed of difficulties, so that you can both be thinking of acceptable alternative answers.**

➤ **Look for specialist organizations, authors and bibliographies of nearly relevant literature, and editors of appropriate periodicals, as possible sources to refer your enquirer to.**

➤ **Consider using information brokers or commercial online services, bearing in mind cost versus value.**

➤ **Make sure that any less detailed or broader substitute answer that you provide still addresses your enquirer's needs.**

Let's end on a positive note. This book is about success, after all. But successful enquiry answering doesn't simply mean handing the answer over with no further comment. It's about making sure that what you provide is the best available, presented to your enquirer in the most helpful way possible. So in the last chapter, we'll look at how to add value.

Chapter 8
Success! Now let's add some value
Presenting your answer well is part of the job

In this chapter you'll find out how to:

➤ make sure that you really have answered the question
➤ decide what to leave out of the answer
➤ take time and trouble over presenting what's left – orally, visually

British catering has long been the butt of comedians. For generations, eating out in Britain was associated with steamed-up windows and soggy cabbage. But things have started changing in recent years. Increasingly, even the most unpretentious little cafés can be pleasant places, with well-prepared food and courteous staff. Why should your library or information unit be any different? They too have been the target of rather cruel humour – not usually deserved – the 'Silence' notices, the fearsome librarians in twinsets and pearls, you know the sort of thing.

Libraries nowadays are much more likely to be bright, modern places with friendly, approachable staff. But there can't be a library in the country that believes it is over-funded. More often than not, the staff are struggling with inadequate resources and the services are struggling with insufficient staff to satisfy the demands placed upon them. That's why the emphasis throughout this book has been on using moderately priced mainstream information sources, and on getting a quart out of a pint pot. Where we have referred to high-priced online services, it has always been on the assumption that they are a medium of last resort.

But you can still take pride in the answers you provide. In helping people find the information they want, you haven't been doing something easy, you've been doing something highly skilled. So don't spoil it by presenting the answer sloppily.

Have you really answered it?

But before you present the answer at all, do make sure that you really have answered the question. Go back to your enquiry form, notebook, log or whatever you use in your library, and check the wording carefully. Do this for two reasons – firstly, because you waste your enquirer's time if you find that you have allowed yourself to be unconsciously diverted during the course of your researches. (Remember your exams again – there are no marks for submitting the perfect answer to a question that isn't on the paper.)

Secondly, you need to check because enquirers are quite capable of changing the agenda while you are searching, without bothering to tell you. Remember the problems you encountered in Chapter 1, trying to find out what your enquirers really wanted in the first place? Unfortunately, it doesn't stop there. While you are busy trying to find the answer, your enquirer is still thinking about the question, and probably coming up with all sorts of supplementary information that they'd like as well. Or they may have been pursuing their own researches in parallel to yours, and have already come up with the answer to the question they originally put to you. Annoying as this may be, you have to be tolerant. After all, it's just a job for you, but it might be personally very important for your enquirer.

What to leave out

We worried about the new phenomenon of information overload as early as Chapter 2. But it's now, while you're preparing to present your answer, that it really matters. You may well have found similar information from several different sources. This could be because you were unhappy with the level of detail in the first directory or statistical source you used, and wanted to see whether you could improve on it in another publication. Or because you found several articles or news features on the same subject, with huge overlaps between them. Or half a dozen different organizations that you could refer your enquirer to, because you hadn't been able to find the information in-house.

But there's no rule that says you have to provide them all. As the quantity of information available continues to grow, enquirers will be looking to information professionals for their expertise not only in finding the right answer but also in judging which is the best *version* of the right answer. There's a rather pretentious saying – 'To govern is to choose'. It implies that making choices is the hardest part of government. It is – it's the hardest part of anything. All information work is about choices – choosing what sources to buy, choosing what index entries to create for them, choosing what to leave out when you write abstracts of them. Why should enquiry work be any different?

Information versus references

Of course, there will be times when you genuinely don't feel well qualified enough to make decisions of this kind – in highly technical subjects such as medicine or law. But even then you can still opt for offering complete texts of only some of the sources, and providing references to the others. That way, you've minimized the amount that your enquirer has to read and, if you've been providing photocopies or downloads of key sources (subject to prevailing copying rules, of course), you've also been kind to trees.

Whatever you decide to provide, you should always tell your enquirer where the information has come from. It may be tempting to keep these details to yourself, in a misguided attempt to ensure that he or she remains dependent on you. But resist the temptation. Firstly, it's a very unprofessional practice for one whose job is information retrieval. Secondly, it's all too easy for an enquirer to go to another library or information unit that is prepared to source its information. And thirdly, if your enquirer subsequently comes back for further details, it's extremely embarrassing if you can't remember where the information came from in the first place.

Presenting what's left

So your task is nearly at an end. You've found the right answer, perhaps in several different forms, and decided which version is the best one for your enquirer's purposes. Now all you have to do is hand it over in triumph. So just take a few moments to decide how you're going to do it. After all, you don't want to spoil the climax, do you?

If you're presenting the answer orally, make sure that what you tell your enquirer covers all the points – no less, no more – and warns of any complications or potential pitfalls. If you're responding by phone, remember too that it will probably take a few seconds for the person at the other end to get onto your wavelength. So use those few seconds to introduce yourself, say where you're calling from and remind the enquirer what s/he asked for. Then check that they've got a pen and paper handy. Then give them the answer. Something like . . .

> Hello, is that Mr Sampson? This is Delilah Milton from the Ghaza Mills Reference Library. You asked me to find Marks & Spencer's current pretax profit, and I have the information for you if you're ready . . . The pretax profit for the year ended 31 March 1999 for Marks & Spencer PLC was £655.7 million. The information comes from the company's own web page. They also announced half year profits of £192.8 million in November 1999. The last full year results were announced in May 1999, which suggests that the 1999–2000 figures could be out very soon. Would you like me to let you know when they appear?

Enhancing answers on paper

When you're presenting an answer on paper, your scope for adding value is enormously enhanced. Obviously if you're simply handing over an original publication, you'll point to the relevant passage or entry. So if you're supplying a photocopy for your enquirer to keep, or if you're faxing the information back, mark the crucial sections. Highlight the relevant paragraph with a marker pen. Put asterisks against the most useful entries in a directory. Draw a line down the required column or across the required row of a table of statistics. Put in an arrow head to point out the key component of a diagram. Circle the right place on a map. And, whatever else you do, make sure that the source of your document is clearly cited. Underline it if it's already printed there; write it in if not. And make sure that all the volume, part and page details are included. These are suggestions, of course, not hard and fast rules. But, as a general principle, do whatever you can to lead your enquirer to the information he or she wants as rapidly and clearly as possible.

Most of your enquiries will probably be quick reference affairs, over and done with in a few minutes. But if you regularly carry out extended enquiry work, why not consider handing over the results in a professional presentation folder? For a fee-based enquiry service, quite a lavish pre-printed offering may well be appropriate – it could enhance the perceived value of the information far beyond the cost of the folder itself. But even for more modest offerings, it could well be worth slipping the papers into a clear plastic folder – costing only a few pence – with a smart piece of stationery, bearing your organization's logo, as the top sheet. And, of course, you'd always include a covering note inviting your enquirer to come back and discuss the outcome if s/he wished.

Word-processing

If you have the opportunity to do some word-processing on the information before you part with it, then your scope for adding value is infinitely increased. This is likely to happen more and more as CD-ROMs replace printed versions of specialist publications, and as you take more information from the web, so you download information instead of simply photocopying it. So help your enquirer to make sense of a large body of text by highlighting the key words or phrases in **bold** or *italic*. Finding those key words or phrases is easy for you; all word-processor packages and web browsers have word-search facilities, so it takes only a few seconds to add an enormous amount of value. Alternatively, you could copy key paragraphs to your clipboard and paste them in at the head of your answer. This allows your enquirer both to take in the crucial information immediately, and also to read it in its proper context later on.

You can enhance statistical information in the same way. If you have downloaded some numeric data to a spreadsheet, then it need be the work of only a few minutes to add value by calculating an average for the figures retrieved, or expressing them as percentages for greater clarity, or ranking them. Or you can turn them into a graph, bar or pie chart. Make sure you really understand what you're doing, though. It's all too easy for simple mistakes in spreadsheet creation to render figures seriously misleading, if not downright wrong!

Copyright, licensing, ethics

Finally, beware. There are ethical considerations to bear in mind when manipulating textual or numeric information in this way. Be sure that you make it quite clear what you have done with the document when presenting it to your enquirer, so that s/he is in no doubt as to how it varies from the original. (And, as always, make sure that you cite the source in full in your answer.) Copyright is a vital issue too. Before you engage in activity of this kind, be sure that you understand the terms on which the software concerned has been licensed to you. If the licence forbids supply of copies to a third party then, no matter how much you may regret the missed opportunity, you must not do it.

As a general principle, in fact, you should make sure that you under-stand *all* the photocopying and downloading restrictions under which your library or information unit operates before you start any enquiry work. There's plenty of help available if you need it; The Library Association, for example, publishes a whole series of copyright guides for different kinds of library, and keeps them up-to-date. As copying in all media becomes easier and easier, publishers rightly become more and more vigilant about infringements. And nothing could be worse for your customer relations than promising something which the rules don't sub-sequently allow you to deliver.

To recap . . .

➤ Check finally that you really have answered the question; it's all too easy to be diverted, or for enquirers to change their mind.

➤ Remember that you don't necessarily have to supply everything you've found; supply the best and refer to the rest.

➤ Make sure you cite sources for every piece of information you supply and, if necessary, indicate how it varies from the original.

➤ Seize every opportunity to add value; compose your oral answers care-fully, highlight key information on paper, word-process downloaded data.

➤ Always make sure you operate within copyright and licensing restrictions.

So that's it! With a little care and common sense – plus a lively and imaginative approach – you can make enquiry answering one of the most satisfying and fulfilling work activities there is. The explosion of available information, the technological developments that can help you retrieve and enhance it, and the enormously increased public awareness of the value of information – all combine to make the prospects for information professionals more exciting than ever before. So the only thing that remains to be done now is to wish you success with your enquiry answering – every time.

Bibliography of key reference sources

Full details of all the twenty-five multi-purpose reference sources listed on page xv, and their international equivalents, appear here – plus a few additional ones that are useful for getting started on a wide range of enquiries. Although nearly all these sources are printed publications, many are also available electronically – on CD-ROM, via online hosts, and increasingly on the web as well. This situation is changing all the time as publishers adapt their titles and content to reflect the requirements and capabilities of the newer media. Where possible, information for this bibliography has been taken from publishers' promotional websites. When investigating any of these sources, I strongly recommend that you visit the publisher's website too, to make sure that you have access to the most up-to-date information available.

Abstracts in new technologies and engineering
Bowker-Saur, Windsor Court, East Grinstead House, East Grinstead, West Sussex RH19 1XA. Tel: 01342 326972 Fax: 01342 336198.
E-mail: custserve@bowker-saur.com
Web: **http://www.bowker-saur.co.uk**
Subject index (with brief abstracts from 1993) to articles in British science and technology periodicals. Companion to *Applied social sciences index & abstracts* and *British humanities index* (q.v.).

Annual abstract of statistics
Office for National Statistics.
The Stationery Office, PO Box 276, London SW8 5DT. Tel: 0870 600 5533. Fax: 0870 600 5522. E-mail: customer.services@theso.co.uk
Web: **http://www.the-stationery-office.co.uk/**
Comprehensive collection of statistics on all subjects, usually abstracted from more detailed government statistical publications.

Annual register
Keesing's Worldwide, 28a Hills Rd, Cambridge CB2 1LA. Tel: 01223 508050. Fax: 01223 508049. E-mail: info@keesings.com

Web: **http://www.keesings.com/**
Provides details of the year's events on a country-by-country basis, plus a political, social and economic overview of each country. Comparable with the much longer *Europa world year book* and with *Statesman's yearbook* (q.v.).

Applied science index & abstracts
H W Wilson Co, c/o Thompson Henry Ltd, London Rd, Sunningdale, Berks SL5 0EP. Tel: 01344 624615. Fax: 01344 626120. E-mail: thl@thompsonhenry.co.uk
Web: **http://www.hwwilson.com/**
Subject index, with abstracts, to articles in English language science and technology periodicals published worldwide. Companion to *General science abstracts*, *Humanities abstracts* and *Social sciences index* (q.v.).

Applied social sciences index and abstracts
Bowker-Saur, Windsor Court, East Grinstead House, East Grinstead, West Sussex RH19 1XA. Tel: 01342 326972. Fax: 01342 336198.
E-mail: custserve@bowker-saur.com
Web: **http://www.bowker-saur.co.uk**
Subject index, with abstracts, to articles in United Kingdom social science periodicals. Companion to *Abstracts in new technologies and engineering* and *British humanities index* (q.v.).

Aslib directory of information sources in the United Kingdom
Aslib, Staple Hall, Stone House Court, London EC3A 7PB. Tel: 020 7903 0000. Fax: 020 7903 0011. E-mail: pubs@aslib.co.uk
Web: **http://www.aslib.co.uk/**
Gives details of services available from special libraries and information units, including terms and conditions for access.

Benn's media
Annual. 3 vols: United Kingdom, Europe, World
Miller Freeman Information Services Ltd, Riverbank House, Angel Lane, Tonbridge, Kent TN9 1SE. Tel: 01732 362666. Fax: 01732 367301. E-mail: scrouch@unmf.com
Web: **http://www.mfplc.co.uk/**
Gives full publication details of periodicals by subject. Competitor to *Willing's Press Guide* (q.v.).

Books in English

British Library, National Bibliographic Service, Boston Spa, Wetherby, West Yorkshire LS23 7BQ. Tel: 01937 546585. Fax: 01937 546586. E-mail: nbs-info@bl.uk

Web: **http://www.bl.uk/**

BLAISE Web: **http://blaiseweb.bl.uk/**

Gives details of every English language title acquired by the British Library and the United States Library of Congress – so effectively covers the whole world.

Bowker/Whitaker global books in print on disc

Bowker-Saur, Windsor Court, East Grinstead House, East Grinstead, West Sussex RH19 1XA. Tel: 01342 326972. Fax: 01342 335612. E-mail: custserve@bowker-saur.com

Web: **http://www.bowker-saur.co.uk**

CD-ROM giving bibliographic details of currently available English language books worldwide. Companion to *International books in print on CD-ROM* (q.v.).

Britain . . . the official yearbook of the United Kingdom

Office for National Statistics.

The Stationery Office, PO Box 276, London SW8 5DT. Tel: 0870 600 5533. Fax: 0870 600 5522. E-mail: customer.services@theso.co.uk

Web: **http://www.the-stationery-office.co.uk/**

Describes British political, social and economic life and gives details of principal United Kingdom institutions.

British humanities index

Bowker-Saur, Windsor Court, East Grinstead House, East Grinstead, West Sussex RH19 1XA. Tel: 01342 326972. Fax: 01342 336198. E-mail: custserve@bowker-saur.com

Web: **http://www.bowker-saur.co.uk**

Subject index (with abstracts from 1991) to articles in British humanities and social science periodicals. Companion to *Abstracts in new technologies and engineering* and *Applied social sciences index & abstracts* (q.v.).

British national bibliography

British Library, National Bibliographic Service, Boston Spa, Wetherby, West Yorkshire LS23 7BQ. Tel: 01937 546585. Fax: 01937 546586. E-mail: nbs-info@bl.uk

Web: **http://www.bl.uk/**
Gives details of all books and pamphlets placed on legal deposit in the British Library, classified by subject.

Centres, bureaux & research institutes
CBD Research Ltd, 15 Wickham Rd, Beckenham, Kent BR3 2JS. Tel: 020 8650 7745. Fax: 020 8650 0768. E-mail: cbdresearch@compuserve.com
Web: **http://www.glen.co.uk/cbd/**
Gives details of United Kingdom centres of expertise. Companion to *Councils, committees & boards, Directory of British associations, Directory of European industrial & trade associations, Directory of European professional & learned societies* and *Pan European associations* (q.v.).

Clover information index
Clover newspaper index
Clover Publications, 32 Ickwell Rd, Northill, Biggleswade, Bedfordshire SG18 9AB. Tel: 01767 627363. Fax: 01767 627004. E-mail: mw@cloverweb.co.uk
Web: **http://www.cloverweb.co.uk/**
Subject indexes to, respectively: articles published in popular British magazines; news items and feature articles published in United Kingdom broadsheet newspapers.

Councils, committees & boards
Current British directories
Directory of British associations & associations in Ireland
Directory of European industrial & trade associations
Directory of European professional & learned societies
CBD Research Ltd, 15 Wickham Rd, Beckenham, Kent BR3 2JS. Tel: 020 8650 7745. Fax: 020 8650 0768. E-mail: cbdresearch@compuserve.com
Web: **http://www.glen.co.uk/cbd/**
Uniform series giving details, respectively, of: official and public bodies and quangos in the United Kingdom; contents of directories and reference works published in the United Kingdom; associations, societies and other organizations throughout the UK and Europe. Companions to *Pan European associations* (q.v.).

Encyclopaedia of associations: international organizations

Gale Group, Watergate House, 13-15 York Buildings, London WC2N 6JU. Tel: 020 7930 3933. Fax: 020 7930 9190. E-mail: globaltech@gale-group.com

Web: **http://www.gale.com/**

Gives details of professional and trade associations, societies and institutions in the United States and elsewhere. Comparable with *Europa directory of international organizations* and *Yearbook of international organizations* (q.v.).

Europa directory of international organisations

Europa world yearbook

Europa Publications Ltd, 18 Bedford Sq, London WC1B 3JN. Tel: 020 7631 3361. Fax: 020 7580 3919. E-mail: sales@europapublications.co.uk

Web: **http://www.europapublications.co.uk/**

Europa directory of international organisations gives details of international and world regional organizations; comparable with *Encyclopaedia of associations: international* (q.v.); competitor to *Yearbook of international organizations* (q.v.). *Europa world yearbook* describes the political, social and economic life of each country of the world, with details of main institutions; comparable with the much shorter *Annual register* and with *Statesman's yearbook* (q.v.). Both companion volumes to *World of learning* (q.v.).

Eurostat: basic statistics of the European Union

Eurostat.

The Stationery Office, PO Box 276, London SW8 5DT. Tel: 0870 600 5533. Fax: 0870 600 5522. E-mail: customer.services@theso.co.uk

Web: **http://www.the-stationery-office.co.uk/**

Eurostat Web: **http://europa.eu.int/eurostat.html**

Comprehensive collection of statistics on all subjects, comparing European Union member states and usually abstracted from more detailed Eurostat publications.

General science abstracts

H W Wilson Co, c/o Thompson Henry Ltd, London Rd, Sunningdale, Berks SL5 0EP. Tel: 01344 624615. Fax: 01344 626120. E-mail: thl@thompsonhenry.co.uk

Web: **http://www.hwwilson.com/**
Subject index, with abstracts, to articles in English language science periodicals published worldwide. Companion to *Applied science index & abstracts*, *Humanities abstracts* and *Social sciences index* (q.v.)
Guide to finding quality information on the Internet
Alison Cooke. Library Association Publishing, 7 Ridgmount St, London WC1E 7AE. Tel: 020 7255 0590. Fax: 020 7255 0591. E-mail: lapublishing@la-hq.org.uk
Web: **http://www.la-hq.org.uk/publishing**
Suggests strategies for locating, selecting and evaluating the quality information on the Net.
Guide to libraries and information units in government departments and other organizations
British Library, Publishing Office, 96 Euston Rd, London NW1 2DB. Tel: 020 7412 7472. Fax: 020 7412 7947. E-mail: paul.wilson@bl.uk
Web: **http://www.bl.uk/**
Gives details of services available from special libraries and information units in United Kingdom government departments and agencies.
Guide to official statistics
Office for National Statistics.
The Stationery Office, PO Box 276, London SW8 5DT. Tel: 0870 600 5533. Fax: 0870 600 5522. E-mail: customer.services@theso.co.uk
Web: **http://www.the-stationery-office.co.uk/**
Explains where to find statistics in British government publications.
Hollis UK press & public relations annual
Hollis Europe: the directory of European public relations & PR networks
Hollis Directories Ltd, Harlequin House, 7 High St, Teddington, Middlesex TW11 8EL. Tel: 020 8977 7711. Fax: 020 8977 1133. E-mail: orders@hollis-pr.co.uk
Web: **http://www.hollis-pr.co.uk/**
Companion volumes giving details of public relations departments and press offices of a very large number of organizations.
Humanities abstracts
H W Wilson Co, c/o Thompson Henry Ltd, London Rd, Sunningdale, Berks SL5 0EP. Tel: 01344 624615. Fax: 01344 626120. E-mail: thl@thompsonhenry.co.uk

Web: **http://www.hwwilson.com/**

Subject index to articles in English language humanities periodicals published worldwide. Companion to *Applied science index & abstracts, General science abstracts* and *Social sciences index* (q.v.)

Instat: international statistics sources: subject guide to sources of comparative international statistics

Routledge, 11 New Fetter Lane, London EC4P 4EE. Tel: 020 7583 9855. Fax: 020 7842 2298. E-mail: info@routledge.com

Web: **http://www.routledge.com/**

Subject index to statistics published by international organizations. Comparable *to Statistics Europe* (q.v.)

Keesing's record of world events

Keesing's Worldwide, 28a Hills Rd, Cambridge CB2 1LA. Tel: 01223 508050. Fax: 01223 508049. E-mail: info@keesings.com

Web: **http://www.keesings.com/**

Provides summaries of news from around the world, with regularly updated subject indexes.

LA copyright guides

(Various titles & editions)

Library Association Publishing, 7 Ridgmount St, London WC1E 7AE. Tel: 020 7255 0590. Fax: 020 7255 0591. E-mail: lapublishing@la-hq.org.uk

Web: **http://www.la-hq.org.uk/publishing**

Series of short guides to copyright law as it applies to various different kinds of library.

Library and information professional's guide to the Internet

Alan Poulter, Debra Hiom, Gwyneth Tseng, Library Association Publishing, 7 Ridgmount St, London WC1E 7AE. Tel: 020 7255 0590. Fax: 020 7255 0591. E-mail: lapublishing@la-hq.org.uk

Web: **http://www.la-hq.org.uk/publishing**

Provides comprehensive guidance on how to use the full range of Internet-based services and facilities.

Pan-European associations

CBD Research Ltd, 15 Wickham Rd, Beckenham, Kent BR3 2JS. Tel: 020 8650 7745. Fax: 020 8650 0768. E-mail: cbdresearch@compuserve.com

Web: **http://www.glen.co.uk/cbd/**
Gives details of Europe-wide professional and trade associations, societies and institutions. Companion to *Centres, bureaux & research institutes*, *Councils, committees & boards*, *Directory of British associations*, *Directory of European industrial & trade associations* and *Directory of European professional & learned societies* (q.v.).

Regional trends
Office for National Statistics.
The Stationery Office, PO Box 276, London SW8 5DT. Tel: 0870 600 5533. Fax: 0870 600 5522. E-mail: customer.services@theso.co.uk
Web: **http://www.the-stationery-office.co.uk/**
Comprehensive collection of statistics on all subjects, comparing each of the United Kingdom standard regions.

Social sciences index
H W Wilson Co, c/o Thompson Henry Ltd, London Rd, Sunningdale, Berks SL5 0EP. Tel: 01344 624615. Fax: 01344 626120. E-mail: thl@thompsonhenry.co.uk
Web: **http://www.hwwilson.com/**
Subject index to articles in English language social science periodicals published worldwide. Companion to *Applied science index & abstracts*, *General science abstracts* and *Humanities abstracts* (q.v.).

Social trends
Office for National Statistics.
The Stationery Office, PO Box 276, London SW8 5DT. Tel: 0870 600 5533. Fax: 0870 600 5522. E-mail: customer.services@theso.co.uk
Web: **http://www.the-stationery-office.co.uk/**
Selection of statistics on a wide range of British social issues, taken from more detailed government statistical publications.

Sources of unofficial UK statistics
Gower Publishing Ltd, Gower House, Croft Rd, Aldershot, Hants GU11 3HR. Tel: 01252 331551. Fax: 01252 344405. E-mail: info@gowerpub.com
Web: **http://www.gowerpub.com**
Gives details of non-governmental statistical sources, mostly relating to business and industry.

Statesman's yearbook
> Macmillan Press Ltd, 25 Eccleston Place, London SW1W 9YY. Tel: 020 7881 8000. E-mail: catherine.jones@macmillan.co.uk
> Web: **http://www.macmillan.co.uk/**
> Describes the political, social and economic life of each country of the world, with details of main institutions. Comparable with the *Annual register* and with the much longer *Europa world yearbook* (q.v.).

Statistics Europe
> CBD Research Ltd, 15 Wickham Rd, Beckenham, Kent BR3 2JS. Tel: 020 8650 7745. Fax: 020 8650 0768. E-mail: cbdresearch@compuserve.com
> Web: **http://www.glen.co.uk/cbd/**
> Subject index to statistical sources published in all European countries. Comparable *to Instat: international statistics sources: subject guide to sources of comparative international statistics* (q.v.)

SubNatStats: a subject index to sub-national statistics
> Research Library, Greater London Authority, 81 Black Prince Rd, London SE1 7SZ. Tel: 020 7787 5500. Fax: 020 7787 5606. E-mail: rlinfo@london-research.gov.uk
> Web: **http://www.london-research.gov.uk/**
> Detailed subject index to contents of United Kingdom statistical sources that include data at regional, local and other sub-national levels

Ulrich's international periodicals directory (incorporating irregular serials & annuals)
> Bowker-Saur, Windsor Court, East Grinstead House, East Grinstead, West Sussex RH19 1XA. Tel: 01342 326972 Fax: 01342 336198. E-mail: custserve@bowker-saur.com
> Web: **http://www.bowker-saur.co.uk**
> Gives details of major periodicals, directories and yearbooks published worldwide by subject.

United Nations Statistical Yearbook
> United National Department for Economic & Social Information. The Stationery Office, PO Box 276, London SW8 5DT. Tel: 0870 600 5533. Fax: 0870 600 5522. E-mail: customer.services@theso.co.uk
> Web: **http://www.the-stationery-office.co.uk/**

United Nations Web: **http://www.un.org/**
Comprehensive collection of statistics on all subjects, comparing most countries of the world.

Walford's guide to reference material
Library Association Publishing, 7 Ridgmount St, London WC1E 7AE. Tel: 020 7255 0590. Fax: 020 7255 0591. E-mail: lapublishing@la-hq.org.uk
Web: **http://www.la-hq.org.uk/lapublishing**
Describes predominantly British reference sources of all kinds on all subjects, including sourcebooks, directories & yearbooks, periodicals, statistics and selected textbooks.

Whitaker's almanac
J Whitaker & Sons Ltd, 12 Dyott St, London WC1A 1DF. Tel: 020 7836 8911. Fax: 020 7836 2909. E-mail: custserve@whitaker.co.uk
Web: **http://www.whitaker.co.uk/**
Comprehensive repository of brief information on all subjects, from a British point of view; a good starting point for information for which there is no obvious specialist source.

Willing's press guide
2 vols: UK & Overseas.
Reed Information Services Ltd, Windsor Court, East Grinstead House, East Grinstead, West Sussex RH19 1XA. Tel: 01342 326972. Fax: 01342 335612. E-mail: jwoodger@reedinfo.co.uk
Web: **http://www.reedinfo.co.uk/**
Gives full publication details of periodicals by subject. Competitor to *Benn's media* (q.v.).

World directory of non-official statistical sources
World marketing data & statistics
Euromonitor plc, 60-61 Britton St, London EC1M 5NA. Tel: 020 7251 8024. Fax: 020 7608 3149. E-mail: info@euromonitor.com
Web: **http://www.euromonitor.com/**
CD-ROMs giving, respectively: references to statistics from non-government sources worldwide (including publications, databases, libraries and market research firms); and demographic, socio-economic and financial facts and figures for countries worldwide.

World of learning

Europa Publications Ltd, 18 Bedford Sq, London WC1B 3JN. Tel: 020 7631 3361. Fax: 020 7580 3919. E-mail: sales@europapublications.co.uk

Web: **http://www.europapublications.co.uk/**

Gives details of universities, colleges, learned societies, research institutes and museums worldwide. Companion to *Europa directory of international organisations* and *Europa world yearbook* (q.v.)

Yearbook of international organizations

Bowker-Saur, Windsor Court, East Grinstead House, East Grinstead, West Sussex RH19 1XA. Tel: 01342 326972 Fax: 01342 336198. E-mail: custserve@bowker-saur.com

Web: **http://www.bowker-saur.co.uk**

Gives contact details and activities of organizations worldwide. Competitor to *Europa directory of international organizations* (q.v.)

Index